Cambridge Ele

C000163779

Elements in Earth System G
edited by
Frank Biermann
Utrecht University
Aarti Gupta
Wageningen University
Michael Mason
London School of Economics and Political Science (LSE)

THE EMERGENCE
OF GEOENGINEERING

*How Knowledge Networks Form
Governance Objects*

Ina Möller
Wageningen University & Research

CAMBRIDGE
UNIVERSITY PRESS

Shaftesbury Road, Cambridge CB2 8EA, United Kingdom

One Liberty Plaza, 20th Floor, New York, NY 10006, USA

477 Williamstown Road, Port Melbourne, VIC 3207, Australia

314–321, 3rd Floor, Plot 3, Splendor Forum, Jasola District Centre,
New Delhi – 110025, India

103 Penang Road, #05–06/07, Visioncrest Commercial, Singapore 238467

Cambridge University Press is part of Cambridge University Press & Assessment,
a department of the University of Cambridge.

We share the University's mission to contribute to society through the pursuit of
education, learning and research at the highest international levels of excellence.

www.cambridge.org
Information on this title: www.cambridge.org/9781009048958

DOI: 10.1017/9781009049696

First published 2023

A catalogue record for this publication is available from the British Library.

ISBN 978-1-009-04895-8 Paperback
ISSN 2631-7818 (online)
ISSN 2631-780X (print)

The Emergence of Geoengineering

How Knowledge Networks Form Governance Objects

Elements in Earth System Governance

DOI: 10.1017/9781009049696
First published online: January 2023

Ina Möller
Wageningen University & Research
Author for correspondence: Ina Möller, ina.moller@wur.nl

Abstract: For many years, suggestions to 'geoengineer' the climate occupied a marginal role in climate change science and politics. Today, visions of massive carbon drawdown and sunlight reflection have become reasonable additions to conventional mitigation and adaptation. Why did researchers start engaging with ideas that were, for a long time, considered highly controversial? And how did some of these ideas come to be perceived worthy of research funding and in need of international governance? This Element provides an analysis of the recent history and evolution of 'geoengineering' as a governance object. It explains how geoengineering evolved from a thought shared by a small network into a governance object that is likely to shape the future of climate politics. In the process, it generates a theory on the earliest phase of the policy cycle and sheds light on the question of why we govern the things we govern in the first place.

Keywords: geoengineering, climate change, governance, history, epistemic community

ISBNs: 9781009048958 (PB), 9781009049696 (OC)
ISSNs: 2631-7818 (online), 2631-780X (print)

Contents

Foreword

My first encounter with geoengineering was in January 2013, when as a graduate student, I read an article by David Victor and colleagues (2009) titled 'The Geoengineering Option: A Last Resort to Global Warming?' The content of the article provided a striking contrast to the sustainability science literature I was used to. It painted a dramatic picture of how climate change would alter the world, how dangerous tipping points would soon be reached, and how governments would not stop carbon emissions any time soon. For these reasons, the authors argued, it was time to look at technological emergency strategies that could curb the effects of global warming. Their plea for more attention to planetary scale solutions was bold and unapologetic, and at the time, both the technology descriptions as well as the confidence with which they promoted them left me with a feeling of foreboding.

I picked up geoengineering again as a research assistant working for the former executive director of the Earth System Governance project, Ruben Zondervan. Ruben was investigating the governance of geoengineering field experiments, and asked me to pull together background information about ongoing activities. My work there led to a PhD position at the Political Science department at Lund University to study geoengineering in a context of institutional complexity. Yet at the time, there were no dedicated institutions, no agreements, no conventions, and I initially felt that there was not much material for an institutional scholar to engage with.

As a PhD student, I gradually honed in on the observation that despite the many drawbacks described by both proponents and critics, geoengineering seemed to be a highly resilient concept. The critical social science scholars I spoke with described it as a sort of whack-a-mole type topic – no matter how often you hit it on the head, it kept popping up again. This got me interested in the constitution and evolution of the idea itself. Where did it come from? How did it travel? And why was it gaining traction, despite all the contestation that it attracted? I wasn't as convinced of the narrative of crisis and political inadequacy that David Victor and colleagues had outlined in their article. Having studied both political and sustainability science, I was aware that environmental and social movements were using a similar narrative to argue for other 'radical' solutions, which didn't seem to gain as much popularity. What then was the deeper story behind geoengineering's apparent success?

It is now almost a decade since I first read David Victor's article. Since then, I have engaged with researchers, activists, and policymakers from many different countries and contexts in the quest to understand how and why geoengineering emerged as a governance object. It is their stories, perspectives, and observations that provide the foundations for this narrative.

Before this background, I bring together my earliest empirical research and latest reflections on the emergence of geoengineering. By tracing the history and social dynamics that shaped the idea, I present my understanding of how and why geoengineering became a governance object. I argue that we need to see geoengineering as one puzzle-piece in a wider setting of economic and environmental policymaking that takes place in a world of unequal power and influence. Seeing geoengineering as such an element of broader scientific and political developments makes it clear that it is not only an emergency plan to save the world from dangerous tipping points. It is also the product of an intricate web of social dynamics that includes the influence of a few authoritative voices, the struggle between different communities of knowledge, and the historical foundations of Western technology and resource exploitation.

1 Introduction

In October 2018, I attended a workshop organized by the German Environment Agency to discuss how the German government should position itself towards geoengineering. At this point, a rumour was circulating that Switzerland would introduce a draft resolution on geoengineering governance at the upcoming United Nations Environment Assembly, and Germany wanted to be prepared. Some key questions at the meeting revolved around who was engaging with and funding geoengineering research, how and where geoengineering was relevant to international law, and what strategies might be used at both national and international levels to ensure that geoengineering did not become a default approach to dealing with climate change. Attendants of the meeting included representatives from the government, civil society, think tanks, and research. I myself had been invited to give a presentation on how to critically read authoritative assessment reports on this subject, as the conveners were sceptical of the policy influence that they perceived to be taking place through these types of publications.

My attendance of the meeting showed me a few important things about the state of geoengineering. One, that it had clearly graduated from being a marginal idea shared by a small group of enthusiasts to becoming a cause of political interest and concern. Two, that the normalization of geoengineering as a policy option was already taking place, and that it was happening through the highest levels of scientific engagement. Three, that (some) policymakers were acutely aware of this process, but that it was difficult to address it in a government setting due to the fragmented nature of the ministerial set-up.

And four, that they perceived geoengineering as being actively pushed for by certain actors, and that they understood this as a problematic sort of lobbying.

Why did geoengineering become an object of governance on the contemporary global science and policy agenda? The most common answer to this question points to the increasing urgency of climate change, the prolonged failure to reduce global greenhouse gas emissions, and the rise in political aspirations (e.g., Parson, 2014; Burns and Nicholson, 2015). While these aspects no doubt played an important role, the question remains why *this* group of techno-scientific approaches seem to have become more mainstream than other 'radical' ideas of addressing climate change (think of a per capita carbon budget, a global carbon tax, or a ban on fossil fuel subsidies). In this Element, I argue that in order to answer this question, we must understand how geoengineering evolved from a marginal idea into a viable policy option discussed in global scientific assessments and political agreements.

Before beginning, I need to point out that many scientists now question the term 'geoengineering' for grouping together technologies that work in fundamentally different ways (see Box 1). In this Element, I nevertheless use it to describe the proposal of addressing climate change by deliberately altering certain components of the Earth's climate system at large scale. Ideas to do this include retroactively removing carbon dioxide and thereby thinning the Earth's layer of greenhouse gases, or actively increasing the Earth's reflectivity in order to reduce the amount of incoming sunlight. Each type of intervention has been proposed as a necessary and feasible mechanism of addressing climate change, and while the procedures of removing carbon or deflecting sunlight are fundamentally different in terms of their physical mechanism, their global orientation, envisioned effect, and design-based perspective can make it useful – from a political perspective – to discuss them under one umbrella term that is seen as separate from conventional mitigation and adaptation.

The emergence of geoengineering on the scientific and political agenda is intriguing for several reasons. First of all, the large-scale modification of natural systems in the name of environmental protection strays substantially from important international norms that have shaped environmental policymaking since the 1970s. In the post-modern era, environmentalism has mostly been associated with reducing human impact, removing man-made sources of pollution, and restoring nature to its 'original' state (Baskin, 2019; Falkner and Buzan, 2019). Most geoengineering technologies, by contrast, aim to strategically increase one human impact on the planet in order to counteract the effects of another. Their normative assumptions about the role and capacity of humankind are thus much more similar to those of the post–world war modernist age, and

Box 1 Geoengineering: A Contested Concept

Geoengineering is usually associated with large-scale and deliberate interventions that aim to moderate climate change. As opposed to conventional mitigation strategies that *avoid* or *prevent* the release of greenhouse gases, geoengineering techniques intend to *reverse* or *counterbalance* the warming effect of emissions that have already been released. In order to achieve this objective, they would need to be deployed at regional or planetary scale.

Ideas on how to do this include removing very large amounts carbon dioxide from the atmosphere and storing it in various forms (carbon dioxide removal (CDR), greenhouse gas removal, negative emissions technologies), or increasing the reflectivity of the planet (solar radiation management (SRM), solar radiation modification, sunlight reflection).

It is important to note that although many small endeavours to remove carbon or reflect sunlight could eventually lead to a reversal or counterbalancing of climate change, the core political concern embodied in the term 'geoengineering' relates to *the idea of being able to engineer planetary systems*. In this Element, geoengineering is thus less about the implications or governance of individual carbon removal or sunlight reflection efforts but more about the consequences of imagining a world in which climate change can be counteracted by deliberate, global interventions.

Still, the wider societal meaning and use of geoengineering has become highly contested. Many scientists nowadays question the use of geoengineering as an umbrella term, seeing it as a diverse set of necessary measures that could help limit global warming, the dangers and merits of which should be discussed individually. For the purpose of designing specific governance mechanisms, this may indeed be true. But for the purpose of a more fundamental discussion of the underlying assumptions that continue to be shared by these measures, I think that the geoengineering umbrella term maintains its merits. In this Element, I thus use the term 'geoengineering' as an anchor with which to trace the evolution of an idea and its relevance to Earth System Governance.

their rise on the agenda reflects a challenge, or 'contestation', of what have long been considered fundamental norms of environmental politics. It thus serves as an interesting case of how this contestation took place.

Second, geoengineering as a concept experienced a remarkable increase in attention and status in a very short amount of time. During the 1990s, the concept existed primarily in the form of an idea sometimes mentioned in the corridors of scientific conferences (Jamieson, 1996).[1] Only few were willing to speak and write about it openly, and those who did expressed their ideas in the form of cautionary 'if', 'should', or 'could' questions (Schneider, 1996). Today, geoengineering policy options occupy central roles in the assessments of many authoritative scientific organizations. Most prominently, they have made it into the projections of the Intergovernmental Panel on Climate Change (IPCC), which include vast amounts of CDR as a way of compensating for anthropogenic greenhouse gas emissions. Even the most controversial form of geoengineering – spraying a layer of reflective sulphur particles across the stratosphere – is openly being considered by renowned scientific bodies like the United States National Academy of Sciences.

Third, the way in which geoengineering technologies are being presented, by some, as feasible and necessary responses to the climate crisis deserves some critical scrutiny. Geoengineering means deliberate intervention into the Earth's ecological systems at planetary scale, and some of the suggestions put forward include degrees of human coordination that have no historical precedent. Deliberately removing atmospheric carbon dioxide at global scale would require nothing less than an industry comparable to contemporary global oil and gas extraction, with potentially enormous consequences for food, energy, and water. Deliberately reflecting sunlight at global scale raises highly complex political questions around decision-making, control, and responsibility in both the short term and the long term. Yet both approaches to global-scale climate management are becoming increasingly discussed as reasonable visions of the future amongst both scientists and policymakers.

In this Element, I examine the trajectory and dynamics that turned geoengineering into a governance object. In Section 2, I trace the origins of geoengineering as a concept and describe the realms of science and politics through which it travelled since the turn of the twenty-first century. In tracing this trajectory, I portray what I see as key moments and debates – sometimes with detailed illustrations, other times with broad brush strokes – while keeping in mind the larger context of ongoing climate politics. In Section 3, I map the knowledge network that evolved around the geoengineering idea. Here I outline the size, shape, and constitution of the network of actors that engaged with geoengineering between 2006 and 2018, highlighting the social dynamics at play in forming, stabilizing, and diffusing it as an object of governance. In Section 4, I reflect on the larger historical and cultural context in which geoengineering arose, discussing how Earth system science, Western colonial

---

[1] The history of geoengineering is much older than this, as I will explain in Section 2.

legacy, and the concept of the Anthropocene created a context in which geoengineering could emerge as a reasonable response to climate change.

My aim with writing this Element is to provide a fresh perspective on geoengineering. To do so, I conceptualize it not as an inevitable outcome of an otherwise failed global climate policy, but as the product of a medium- and long-term political and social process. I hope that by explaining the emergence of geoengineering, decision-makers can contextualize geoengineering as an idea that developed in a specific political, social, cultural, and historical context and take this into account when deciding how to engage with it.

1.1 Governance Objects and Knowledge Networks

For the purpose of tracing the emergence of geoengineering, I conceptualize the idea as a 'governance object' (Corry, 2013). The term governance object describes an idea or concept (from 'ecosystem services' to 'women's rights') that becomes subject to political decision-making at any level. It highlights how the creation and shape of a politically relevant concept affects the resulting politics around it, and that this shape is itself determined by political processes in which social actors are involved. As Bentley Allan (2017, p. 133) argues, 'the production of governance objects is neither natural nor inevitable and has important effects on how global problems are understood and governed'. In his seminal article, he explains how even the widely taken-for-granted governance object of 'climate change' has been constructed in a social process, highlighting how particular moments of interaction between state and scientific actors resulted in a geophysical definition of the governance object rather than a bioecological one.

Rather than assuming that governance objects are simply out there and waiting to be put onto a global agenda, this perspective emphasizes the discursive and social processes by which a governance object must first be created. Olaf Corry (2013) theorizes the origins of a governance object as a process in which an object is first designated, or defined, as being separate from other objects (distinctiveness), then problematized with respect to globally relevant interests and frames (saliency), and finally translated into a portable, global object that can be used in contexts around the world (malleability). Only after a governance object is thus constituted can it emerge as an issue and be taken up by the agenda-setting actors described in other influential models of the global policy cycle (e.g., Finnemore and Sikkink, 1998).

In terms of identifying where such a governance object might originate, I draw inspiration from the many scholars of environmental politics who study transnational knowledge networks. The concept of a knowledge network marries the literature on 'epistemic communities' (Haas, 1992b) and 'transnational advocacy networks' (Keck and Sikkink, 1999). Diane Stone (2002, p. 2) describes them as networks that 'incorporate professional associations, academic research groups and scientific communities that organize around a special subject matter or issue'. While many such knowledge networks engage in the disinterested pursuit of knowledge, some are also focused on influencing policy and can include actors that range from universities over philanthropic organizations to non-governmental organizations and pressure groups.

The concept of a knowledge network thus explicitly combines the notion of a science and an advocacy network. As Mai'A Davis Cross (2013) notes, most of the literature on science networks or 'epistemic communities' has been unnecessarily narrow in its empirical focus on groups of scientists and their efforts to influence governments. The wider literature on transnational networks shows that different types of expert communities can exist and interact within the same knowledge network, that they have an active role in shaping global governance processes, and that they influence the views of both state and non-state actors. Andreas Antoniades (2003) further explains that rather than just communicating knowledge to power, these communities' principal mode of influence is the *construction of social reality*. Because of their authoritative knowledge basis, they have the power to impose discourses about what should be considered a problem. While the communities themselves are not independent of already existing discourses and structures, their position as recognized makers of knowledge gives them preferential access to the language that shapes social reality. This access to language brings us back to the theory on governance objects described in Corry (2013). Designating a problem, highlighting its relevance, and making sure it is globally transportable is a task tailored to the skills and capacities of knowledge networks.

How do knowledge networks produce global governance objects? The literature provides us with multiple conditions under which different communities within such a knowledge network are likely to influence policymaking, but still struggles with explaining the mechanisms that might lead to these conditions. Thus, Peter Haas (1992a) has highlighted the degree of consensus within a community and its access to policymakers in a phase of political uncertainty as principal determinants of its success. Mai'A Davis Cross (2013) summarizes additional scope conditions that scholars have identified as being likely to increase a community's influence. These include activity in the early phase of the policy process, compatibility with existing institutional norms, study of quantitative data and/or natural systems, and weakness of competing communities. So far, these conditions are mostly treated as exogenous and are rarely linked to internal social dynamics of the community or wider knowledge network itself. But could it be that they are in fact interdependent outcomes of more fundamental characteristics that define a certain type of knowledge network, namely one that is capable of producing a global governance object?

What happens if, instead of thinking of two separate entities, we conceptualize the knowledge network and the governance object as one co-evolving amalgam of community and discourse? If we re-imagine knowledge networks as the *source* of global governance objects, then the facilitating conditions of uncertainty and activity in the early phase of the policy process are no longer scope conditions; they are embedded in the fact that the knowledge network itself is creating a new governance object. Also the compatibility with existing institutional norms is not exogenous. Deliberate catering to certain narratives is just as important for the success of a governance object as is the creation of the object itself. This may also explain why the engagement with quantitative data and/or natural systems is considered a facilitating condition. Given the contemporary attribution of authority to numbers and science in Western governance, communities that choose to use quantitative methods may be more successful at catering to the interests and needs of policymakers. The role of competition between communities can also take on new meaning if we see it as adding to increase of distinctiveness, salience, and malleability of a governance object. Rather than just considering the 'strength' or 'weakness' of different communities, we might do well to focus more on their interaction.

1.2 Studying the Emergence of Geoengineering

In studying geoengineering as an amalgam of community and discourse, I focus on the causal mechanisms that characterize the concept's emergence. The study of causal mechanisms is summarized in the book of Alexander George and Andrew Bennett (2005) on case studies as a way to 'open up the black boxes of nature to reveal their inner workings' and 'exhibit the ways in which the things we want to explain come about' (p. 135). To open up this 'black box' around the emergence of geoengineering, I rely mainly on process tracing, supported by document analysis, social network analysis, participant observations, and interviews as input data.

Process tracing amounts to 'the systematic examination of diagnostic evidence selected and analysed in the light of research questions and hypotheses posed by the investigator' (Collier, 2011, p. 823). Choosing what diagnostic evidence to look at is dependent on the researcher's knowledge of the case, including awareness of recurring empirical regularities and the use of an explanatory model. This means beginning with a certain event and tracing the historical pathway through which the event emerged. It also provides an analytical explanation that is 'couched in theoretical variables that have been identified in a research design' (Bennett and George, 1997, p. 6).

Effectively, this entire Element relies on process tracing to understand the emergence of geoengineering as a governance object. It starts with describing the historical trajectory of geoengineering since the turn of the twenty-first century, including insights from document analysis, observations, and interviews (Section 2). It then focuses on the analytical explanation of how geoengineering became an object of governance, distilling specific social dynamics by which the geoengineering concept and the community around it co-constituted each other (Section 3). Finally, it reflects on larger contextual factors that facilitated the emergence of geoengineering as a governance object (Section 4).

To support this process tracing endeavour, document analysis served as a way to analyze the evolution of the geoengineering concept. This was an iterative procedure in which I read contemporary studies on geoengineering, identified the studies that were highly cited, reverse-snowballed to sources that those highly cited studies referred to, and assessed the referred studies in comparison to other studies addressing the same issue and published within a similar time frame. This confirmed that authoritative assessment reports act as major influencers on the streamlining of an idea and contribute to ordering a previously contested discussion. For this reason, key authoritative assessment reports are highlighted throughout the analysis in Section 2.

Social network analysis served as a way to draw a boundary around the geoengineering epistemic community, to identify which actors and organizations were actively engaged in the community, and which individuals seem to have played an important role. It is a method used to map actors and their social relations and a way to uncover underlying patterns of interactions and relations in groups (Borgatti et al., 2009). To determine the boundaries of the geoengineering knowledge network, I used the programmes of geoengineering workshops and conferences, reasoning that those who make the effort to repeatedly attend and present at such events demonstrate significant dedication to the group. This kind of event data provides an opportunity to capture those members of the network who are not scholars or academics and provides additional insights to publication-based network analyses, such as those conducted by Belter and Seidel (2013) and Oldham et al., (2014). It can also trace participation and connections over time, providing an advantage over survey-based data. The results of this analysis are reported primarily in Section 3.

Observations and interviews served as a way to gain access to the perceptions of people involved with geoengineering research, both at the core and at its fringes. Much of the data gathered for this stage can be considered ethno-graphic, as described by Guest et al., (2013). By getting to know the people in the network, engaging in professional conversations and following the main debates over several years, I developed an in-depth understanding of the language and dynamics used within the community. This helped to gain access to events, researchers, and external observers. I was thus able to share experi-ences with interviewees and conversation partners, enabling deeper reflexivity and contextualization than if I had stayed completely outside the community and collected data through surveys or structured questionnaires. Furthermore, it helped me understand some of the core conflicts, dilemmas, and motivations that shape the geoengineering community. These insights flow into Sections 2, 3, and 4.

1.3 Reflections on Theory and Method

All studies are subject to theoretical and methodological limitations, and this one is no exception. In the following, I point out some considerations that the reader needs to be aware of when drawing conclusions from this Element.

The first consideration is that because I employ a constructivist perspective, I assume all types of knowledge, including scientific knowledge, are socially constructed. In this perspective, climate science is a knowledge system like many others that is governed by its own rules, norms, and politics (Beck et al., 2014; Lövbrand et al., 2015; Allan, 2017). Studying the social dynamics that govern scientific knowledge production is an enterprise that I share with other scholars of science and society, and that contributes to improving our under-standing of why we govern geoengineering in the way we do (Asayama et al., 2019; Low and Schäfer, 2019; Kreuter, 2021; Oomen, 2021; Schubert, 2021). This perspective does not, in any way, intend to undermine or discard the value of science. Rather, it recognizes science as an authoritative and powerful kind of knowledge that, like any other sources of power, deserves critical analysis in order to ensure that this power is used in a reflexive, responsible, and transpar-ent manner.

The second consideration is that in studying geoengineering as a socially constructed governance object, I place more emphasis on its ideational nature and social context than on its underlying materiality. This materiality is, how-ever, an important factor for explaining how geoengineering emerged on the political agenda. It is even more important for recognizing the often unques-tioned trajectories that we are on and the alternatives that might exist. For these reasons, I explore some aspects of geoengineering's underlying materiality in Sections 2 and 4, where I briefly discuss the role of scenarios, computers, and models in helping to conceptualize the planet as an object that can be modified at will. Yet these are only limited explorations, and I would encourage any future studies on the emergence of geoengineering or similar governance objects to focus more explicitly on the role and power of such material factors.

The third consideration is that although process tracing allows me to provide a narrative of how geoengineering emerged as a governance object, such a narrative will always be influenced by my own experiences, perspectives, and interpretations. There may be aspects of the story that I have missed out on or that I understand in a different way than others do. It is very likely that not all perspectives are represented, as I have had more access to some accounts than to others. To compensate for this, I have made sure to integrate multiple types of data. In being transparent about the sources I use and the approach I take, I hope the readers of this Element will acknowledge this limitation and still take something useful from this narrative.

Finally, my narrative employs a few specific methods that are subject to limitations of their own. In using a snowball-type document analysis, my analysis of the geoengineering literature focuses on studies that are known and cited within the geoengineering knowledge network. This means they are published in English and most often written by people linked to that knowledge network. Other studies, using other terms or languages and written by individuals who are further removed from the network, are not taken into account. This limitation is also reflected in my use of network analysis. Because I use conference attendance lists to map out the geoengineering knowledge network, my study focuses on the community of scholars who attended these conferences. Other groups that may exist or work independently from this community are less central to this Element, although some (like the community of integrated assessment modellers, or the community of civil society actors who oppose geoengineering research) are included as important protagonists in the narrative. My observations of the knowledge network have also mostly been as an observer at the fringe of the community and do not compare to the kind of in-depth ethnographic work that has been conducted by others in this field (e.g., Gannon and Hulme, 2018; Buck, 2019; Oomen, 2021). This means that my account of individual narratives and understandings is less detailed, but also that I try to provide insights into a wider range of perspectives.

2 Tracing the Geoengineering Trajectory

Although this Element dedicates itself to explaining the emergence of geoengineering on the contemporary scientific and political agenda, I first need to point out that the idea itself is much older than the recent time period that I focus on – at least as old as climate science itself. Julia Schubert (2021, 2022) has recently written a couple of excellent reviews and analyses of this history, the likes of which I will not reproduce here. Suffice to say that deliberate climate modification was long seen as a promising tool to improve the condition of humankind, with global warming itself initially regarded as a desirable development. At the turn of the twentieth century, even the renowned Swedish climatologist Svante Arrhenius speculated how burning coal might lead to a virtuous cycle of global warming, arguing that in this cycle 'we may hope to enjoy ages with more equable and better climates . . . when the earth will bring forth more abundant crops than at present' (Arrhenius, 1908, p. 63).

Global warming only came to be seen as a problem in need for response in the 1960s, and at this point, the first instinct was to address it with some sort of global counter-engineering. In 1965, the White House published a report on environmental pollution in which it recommends the exploration of 'counter-vailing climatic changes' to address rising temperatures, including spreading reflective particles over the oceans or engineering cirrus clouds (President's Science Advisory Committee, 1965, p. 127). In 1977, a physicist and systems modeller by the name of Cesare Marchetti, who was then working at the International Institute for Applied Systems Analysis (IIASA) in Austria, first introduced the term 'geoengineering' in relation to climate change. His suggestion was to address the 'CO_2 problem' by disposing captured emissions in the deep ocean using ocean currents (Marchetti, 1977). But such ideas came into disfavour with the rise of environmental movements in the 1970s and 1980s, which questioned the narrative of modernity and industrialism and gave rise to the precautionary environmental norms that we are familiar with today. As Schubert (2021, p. 28) argues, at this time, geoengineering 'did not gain, but rather lost currency in the face of political concerns over climate change'.

2.1 (Re-)claiming the Climate Policy Portfolio

Beneath the radar of political environmentalism, the geoengineering idea lingered on. In the early 1980s, a committee under the United States National Research Council published a report for Congress titled 'Changing Climate' (Nierenberg et al., 1983). Among the members of this committee were Thomas Schelling and William Nordhaus, two prominent economists who played decisive roles in shaping the security and climate policies of the United States. At the time, Schelling's realist perspective on game theory, conflict strategy, and bargaining formed the backbone of US nuclear deterrence politics, while Nordhaus' market liberal perspective on relative gains and the preference for high discount rates (i.e., attributing low importance to costs for future generations) was shaping the core of contemporary integrated assessment models (IAMs). The perspectives that these committee members brought to the table influenced the report's suggestions on how to address the problem of climate change. In reaction to earlier reports that emphasized the need to conserve fossil fuels and switch to cleaner energy sources, the authors argued that it would be wrong to see prevention of climate change as the only or most appropriate policy response. They argued that although there was a widespread methodological preference for dealing with causes rather than symptoms,

> it may be wrong to commit ourselves to the principle that, if fossil fuels and CO_2 are where the problem lies, they must also be where the solution lies. ... Defining the issue as 'the CO_2 problem' can focus attention too exclusively on energy and fossil fuels and divert it from rainfall or irrigation or, more even-handedly, the broad issue of climate change. (Nierenberg et al., 1983, p. 56)

Throughout the National Research Council chapter, it is conspicuous how the authors diverted attention from the energy industry and instead advocated for improving water management and agricultural practices. Perhaps it is worth mentioning that the oil and gas giant Exxon Corporation had written an internal memo on the CO_2 greenhouse effect just one year earlier, in which it not only fully recognized the connection between fossil fuels and increasing temperatures, but also predicted that a doubling of the current concentration would lead to average warming of up to 3.1°C (unevenly distributed, with up to 10°C warming at the poles). It also acknowledged that mitigating the greenhouse gas effect would require 'major reductions in fossil fuel combustion', while shifting between fossil fuels was not an option. Despite acknowledging this, the memo concluded that '[m]aking significant changes in energy consumption patterns now to deal with this potential problem amid all the scientific uncertainties would be premature in view of the severe impact such moves could have on the world's economies and societies'. (Exxon research and engineering company, 1982, p. 2)

By chance or not, the National Research Council report on 'Changing Climate' ended up arguing along very similar lines.

Pointing out the uncertainties that remained, the difficulties that reducing fossil fuel consumption would entail, and the potential benefits that climate change could bring, the National Research Council committee essentially warned against any immediate action to 'solve the CO_2 problem' (Nierenberg et al., 1983, p. 63). Instead, Schelling proposed a framework that could account for a variety of future preferences and possibilities, and that supplemented emissions cut with three additional types of responses: CDR from the ambient atmosphere; adaptation through changes in agricultural practices, migration, and compensation; and the deliberate modification of climate and weather. He later went on to argue that 'geoengineering', as global climate modification came to be known, would immensely simplify climate change policy by circumventing the dependency on behavioural change, national regulations, and universal participation. Instead, it would merely involve 'deciding what to do, how much to do, and who is to pay for it' (Schelling, 1996, p. 303).

Meanwhile, international concern about global warming grew stronger. Based on the success of the recently adopted Montreal Protocol for the protection of the Ozone layer, trust in science, international institutions and global markets to address global environmental problems was at an all-time high (Oberthür, 2001). On 6 December 1988, the United Nations General Assembly called on the World Meteorological Organization and the United Nations Environment Programme to prepare a comprehensive review of the state of knowledge on climate change, its impacts on the economy and society, and on possible response strategies. The first report of the resulting IPCC played a key role in affirming human impact on the climate, and highlighted the need to reduce emissions from human activities by over 60 per cent in order to stabilize concentrations at contemporary levels (IPCC, 1990). Two years later, the international community adopted the United Nations Framework Convention on Climate Change, in which parties agreed to 'take precautionary measures to anticipate, prevent or minimize the causes of climate change', stating that a lack of scientific certainty should not be used as a reason to postpone such measures (UNFCCC, 1992, p. 4).

The agreement was operationalized through the adoption of the Kyoto Protocol in 1997, committing developed countries to limit greenhouse gases according to pre-defined individual targets. A key aspect of the negotiations in preparation of the protocol was the inclusion of carbon sinks as an accepted method to offset emissions. The United States and other countries of the so-called Umbrella group (comprising, amongst others, the United States, Canada, Russia, Australia, Norway, and New Zealand) had lobbied to include the active maintenance of forests as a way to offset emissions that were generated through changes of land use (there was no talk yet of offsetting industrial emissions through sinks). At that point, most other parties to the UNFCCC – including the European Union, China, and many developing countries – were sceptical of the idea to include sinks as a way of mitigating climate change. China and the G77 opposed the proposal by raising concerns that through sinks, the United States could effectively 'cheat' on its commitment to emissions reductions. However, they did not succeed in stopping the proposal (Boyd et al., 2008). In addition, and again at the behest of the United States, the protocol also established an elaborate carbon trading scheme. Although countries were supposed to focus first and foremost on reducing national emissions, the carbon market gave them the possibility to offset (some of) their emissions by investing in clean energy and carbon removal projects elsewhere, including in developing countries (Matsuo, 2003).

While at the international level countries were preparing and negotiating the contents of the climate convention, geoengineering re-appeared on the US policy agenda. In January 1992, the National Academy of Sciences (NAS) released another report on climate policy options for US congress (National Academy of Sciences, 1992). Robert Frosch, the then vice president for research at General Motors and scientific member of the responsible NAS panel, had vociferously argued for including a chapter on geoengineering options that included large-scale afforestation, ocean fertilization, marine cloud brightening, and dispersion of dust in the stratosphere as potential alternatives or add-ons to climate change mitigation. As others would do later on, Frosch justified the inclusion of such a chapter with the argument that humanity was already engaging in a form of inadvertent geoengineering, and that a radical reduction of greenhouse gas emissions would imply severe consequences for the (fossil fuel-based) economy. Stephen Schneider, then working at the US National Center for Atmospheric Research, writes that at the time, the inclusion of this chapter was highly controversial:

> As a member of that panel, I can report that the very idea of including a chapter on geoengineering led to serious internal and external debates. Many participants (including myself) were worried that even the very thought that we could offset some aspects of inadvertent climate modification by deliberate climate modification schemes could be used as an excuse by those who would be negatively affected by controls on the human appetite to continue polluting and using the atmosphere as a free sewer. (Schneider, 1996, p. 295)

Although the chapter was eventually approved, the widely held normative emphasis on reducing human impact to protect the environment continued making the idea of geoengineering unpopular, and so only a handful of scientists were engaging with it. From the 1990s to the mid-2000s, active research took place mainly in the field of ocean fertilization. Marine research groups from the United States, Germany, the United Kingdom, Canada, New Zealand, India, and Japan were conducting a row of scientific experiments that tried to establish the role of iron in the climate cycle. Their interest derived from a hypothesis set up by John Martin from California's Moss Landings Marine Laboratories in 1990, suggesting that an increase of iron-rich dust to certain parts of the ocean would increase algae growth and that this in turn might remove carbon dioxide from surface waters and enhance the ocean's capacity to absorb more CO_2 from the atmosphere (Martin, 1990). Proof for this hypothesis remained inconclusive, and scientific experimentation on ocean fertilization ceased (for at least a decade) in 2009.[2] The last scientific experiment to be conducted with ocean fertilization in this period was a German–Indian collaboration under the project name LOHAFEX. Under this initiative, scientists fertilized 300 km[2] of the Southern Ocean with six tons of dissolved iron. This experiment was branded as a dangerous 'geoengineering project' by advocacy groups and attracted major international criticism, leading to a discontinuation of this kind of research soon after (Bundesregierung, 2012; Oomen, 2021). But beyond these experiments, research on large-scale climate intervention largely remained beneath the radar of public interest.

Scientific interest in geoengineering changed decisively in the period between 2006 and 2008, where bibliometric analyses show a sudden increase in the amount of publications that dealt with geoengineering (Belter and Seidel, 2013; Oldham et al., 2014). A row of articles on geoengineering technologies published in the journal *Climatic Change* included an opinion piece by Nobel Prize-winning atmospheric chemist Paul Crutzen (2006). Crutzen argued that despite emissions reductions being by far the most preferred approach to address climate change, atmospheric carbon dioxide was still increasing. Because of this, he advocated for the re-examination of stratospheric aerosol injection as a possible (though suboptimal) contribution to solving the climate change problem. Though Crutzen was not the first to suggest or discuss stratospheric aerosol injection, his reputation and international standing is often cited as one reason for why geoengineering research experienced a sudden boost in confidence (Lawrence and Crutzen, 2017).

Another reason for the increase in attention was the involvement of private actors in the field of ocean fertilization. In 2007, the US-based and publicly traded company Planktos Corporation announced that it was planning to fertilize 10,000 km[2] off the coast of the Galapagos Islands, aiming to generate credits for the international carbon offsetting market. At the time, media was framing iron fertilization as a possible solution to climate change, and early movers like Planktos saw a potential to make profit by selling cheap credits to countries who were looking to offset their carbon emissions. The company's announcements were countered by an unexpected outrage campaign. Branding Planktos' ocean fertilization plans as 'geoengineering', a transnational coalition of civil society organizations including Greenpeace, the ETC Group, and the International

---

[2] Ocean fertilization has recently found a revival in scientific interest. Since 2019, a consortium of mainly European research institutes are working on enhancing the alkalinity of oceans by adding lime and therefore modifying the ocean's capacity to absorb carbon dioxide under the EU-funded OceanNETs project (OceanNETs, 2022).

Union for Conservation of Nature emphasized the risks of ocean iron fertilization by presenting critical research papers to the Convention on Biological Diversity and the London Convention on marine dumping, thereby bringing the case into the realm of international environmental law (Fuentes-George, 2017). In response to these NGO campaigns around the Planktos case and an actual example of privately led ocean iron fertilization off of the coast of British Columbia in 2012, the Convention on Biological Diversity and the London Protocol introduced restrictive guidelines on when and under what circumstances 'geoengineering' and 'marine geoengineering' experiments could be allowed (Ginzky and Frost, 2014; Fuentes-George, 2017).

2.2 The Road to 'Net Zero'

Meanwhile in the realm of international climate negotiations, countries were under pressure to form an international agreement that would supersede the Kyoto Protocol, scheduled to expire in 2012. The failure of the 2009 climate conference in Copenhagen to produce such an agreement had added to the already widespread critique of what was considered a 'malfunctioning' Kyoto Protocol, and dashed hopes that international negotiations would succeed at reaching a sustainable and long-term solution to climate change. In this situation, it was critical to reach a diplomatic success in order to counteract widespread feelings of hopelessness and resignation.

For many years, the European Union had seen itself as a front runner of ambitious climate policy and had continuously advocated for an international agreement to remain below 2°C average global warming (Parker et al., 2017). At the same time, the Alliance of Small Island States was playing a strong advocacy role in also considering 1.5°C as a possible long-term temperature target, due to the immediate threats from sea-level rise that low-lying island states would otherwise face (Benjamin and Thomas, 2016). Though the two groups of countries eventually succeeded in introducing these targets to the global climate negotiations, they also faced international pressure to demonstrate that such stringent targets were still feasible and credible.

In search for support, the responsible political bodies of the European Commission turned to science for confirmation. In a series of interactions between EU officials and a large-scale European research programme on adaptation and mitigation strategies, the involved scientists were encouraged to focus their efforts on modelling scenarios that showed the technical feasibility of remaining below 2°C (Lövbrand, 2011). Summarized under the acronym 'RCPs' (Representative Concentration Pathways), the resulting scenarios became the 'backbone' of the fifth assessment report of the IPCC (van Beek et al., 2020).

These RCPs took a different approach to scenario development than what had previously been done in the IPCC under the SRES (Special Report on Emissions Scenarios) approach.[3] While the SRES scenarios had used assumptions about social change to *forecast* a range of possible societal futures impacted by climate change, the RCPs used certain levels of radiative forcing (translated to temperature targets) to *back-cast* a range of possible policy pathways to avoid impact from climate change (Oreskes, 2015). This meant that it was now up to the model to decide which combination of policy approaches would be most feasible to reach the pre-defined target.

Important to explain here is the functioning of IAMs used to calculate the RCP scenarios. Integrated assessment models are rather complex combinations of physical science and economic climate models, and many of the assumptions that go into them are relatively opaque. The economic side is built according to mainstream economic theories, in which cost minimization is the key factor for choice of mitigation method and in which carbon price is the main incentive (Carton, 2021). Even more significantly, IAMs generally rely on high discount rates (3.5–5 per cent), meaning that costs to be covered in the future are significantly cheaper than costs that need to be covered in the present. This leads to a preference for future policies if such policies are available to the model (Köberle, 2019). Over the years, the physical science side of these IAMs developed towards focusing on atmospheric concentrations of carbon dioxide, expressing climate targets in terms of 'parts per million' (ppm) and later in terms of a cumulative carbon budget. The IAMs also emphasize technological promises over any kind of transformative societal or economic change, a trend that has reproduced itself throughout the history of climate change modelling and policy. For this reason, both climate science and climate policy have tended to focus largely on (technological) approaches like energy efficiency, nuclear power, and carbon capture and storage (CCS) as preferred policies to dealing with climate change (McLaren and Markusson, 2020).

Complying with the EU commission's call for low-temperature scenarios, the RCPs introduced the new idea that while calculating the remaining carbon budget, it was possible to go 'net-negative'. This meant projecting a future scenario (known as RCP 2.6) where the world could absorb more carbon dioxide than it was producing (Anderson and Peters, 2016). In order to do so, the underlying IAMs drew heavily on a technology that had already been

---

[3] The SRES scenarios were supposed to be replaced with updated version called 'Shared Socio-Economic Pathways' (SSPs) that would become part of an integrated climate assessment in tandem with the RCPs. The development of these had, however, been delayed, and so the RCPs became the centre of attention in AR5 (Cointe *et al.*, 2019). Only by AR6 were the SSPs ready, and now provide a set of 'baseline worlds' which are in turn used to generate new RCPs.

suggested as a way to reduce the costs of mitigation in the IPCC's fourth assessment report: Bioenergy with Carbon Capture and Storage (BECCS) (McLaren and Markusson, 2020).

Combining bioenergy with the (still speculative) technology of CCS had been proposed in the early 2000s by climate modellers at the IIASA in Austria (the same institute at which Cesare Marchetti had first used the term geoengineering in 1977). The researchers had argued that, under the precautionary principle, the portfolio of technological options needed to be spread in order to reduce climate risk (Obersteiner, 2001). They presented BECCS as a reliable and permanent form of terrestrial carbon sink that could 'neutralize unsustainable historical carbon emissions in the course of a century' (Kraxner et al., 2003, p. 286). Although the technology did not exist yet, it was presented a reasonable hypothetical possibility that matched well with the economic, physical, and technology-oriented assumptions of the IAMs.

The RCP 2.6 and its use of BECCS assured policymakers that the 2°C target was technically feasible, and played a key role in the preparations for the 2015 climate conference in Paris and in its eventual success (Beck and Mahony, 2017). At that point, the concept of 'net zero' was already circulating in the IAM and policy community. Joeri Rogelj, a prominent climate modeller based at IIASA, had introduced the term 'net zero' to the 2014 UNEP Emissions Gap Report and highlighted it as the most useful way of conceptualizing long-term emissions targets (Rogelj et al., 2015). In his 2015 paper, he draws on a 2008 publication by Damon Matthews and Ken Caldeira (whom we will meet again later in the context of solar geoengineering), in which the authors write that 'to achieve atmospheric carbon dioxide levels that lead to climate stabilization, the *net* addition of CO_2 to the atmosphere from human activities must be decreased to nearly *zero*' (Matthews and Caldeira, 2008, own emphasis).

Picking up the 'net zero' term, the previously mentioned Umbrella group again lobbied to make the use of carbon sinks central to the objective of climate change mitigation. During the 2014 UNFCCC climate meeting in Lima, New Zealand, supported by Switzerland, first brought 'net zero' to the negotiation table. Norway and the United States suggested comparable terms, including 'carbon neutrality' and 'decarbonization of the global economy' (Dooley and Gupta, 2017). Parallel efforts were made by a group of influential diplomats, who had identified 'net zero' emissions as a practical and stringent target relevant to the policies of individual countries (Darby, 2019). But as developing countries were wary of introducing new concepts, 'net zero' was eventually replaced with language already known in the UNFCCC context and became what is now the widely cited Article 4.1 of the Paris Agreement: the balancing of anthropogenic sources and sinks (Dooley and Gupta, 2017).

The idea of 'net zero' and RCP 2.6's option of going net-negative opened up a world of possibilities, including the acceptability of a so-called overshoot scenario. Allowing for overshoot meant that the world could go beyond the limit of 450 ppm carbon dioxide concentration that the IAMs associated with remaining below 2°C, if only it deployed enough negative emissions technologies to remove the excessive amounts of greenhouse gases in the long term. Given this possibility, and as a result of the Paris Agreement's adoption of the 2°C and 1.5° C targets, the scientific community was again tasked with evaluating emissions pathways that were compatible with the envisioned (even lower) temperature goals. Though many scientists were deeply sceptical about the feasibility of such ambitious levels of mitigation, the IPCC accepted the invitation and published its special report on 1.5°C in 2018 (Livingston and Rummukainen, 2020). Again, it presented a set of pathways that assured the possibility of staying below 1.5°C – provided that the world managed to deploy a variety of negative emissions technologies at a scale that paralleled the contemporary expanse of the fossil fuel industry. At this point, it also officially adopted the term 'net zero' and made it the preferred term in official climate policy vocabulary. Yet while net zero neatly communicated a necessity to reach a balance between anthropogenic emissions and removals, it did not say much about how to practically achieve this.

In the meantime, 'net zero' has generated an unprecedented groundswell of seemingly ambitious climate pledges by public and corporate actors, under the assumption that the use of negative emissions technologies is not only possible, but also a necessary component of climate policymaking. Yet to what extent these will be met by actually reducing emissions, rather than relying on the large-scale deployment of CDR techniques, is still unclear. In a stock-take of existing 'net zero' targets, researchers from the Energy and Climate Intelligence Unit and Oxford University found that by the end of 2020, 61 per cent of global emissions had been addressed through net zero targets. However, only 20 per cent of these met a minimum level of robustness criteria, and the degree to which the analyzed actors intend to rely on greenhouse gas offsetting remained mostly unspecified (Black et al., 2021). A more recent report by the New Climate Institute and Carbon Market Watch gives a scathing review of the world's twenty-five largest companies' climate targets, showing how their 'net zero' pledges commit to only about 40 per cent reduction in emissions, as opposed to the 100 per cent suggested by their claims to carbon neutrality (New Climate Institute, 2022).

Many onlookers are deeply concerned that the vagueness around reliance on negative emissions could endanger the focus on need for short-term climate action and place unrealistic expectations in the amount of resources available to absorb excess carbon dioxide (Jones, 2018; Markusson et al., 2018; Carton, 2019;

McLaren et al., 2019; Workman et al., 2020). Key to this is the understanding that negative emissions technologies were originally meant to absorb emissions that are considered extremely difficult to mitigate (so-called residual emissions). This means that negative emissions technologies such as afforestation or BECCS would be needed *in addition to* stringent emissions cuts in all sectors, in order to offset unavoidable emissions from changes in land use. If, however, 'negative emissions' are seen as equivalent to the 'positive emissions' produced by burning fossil fuels and relied upon to make greenhouse gas-intensive industries like oil recovery and usage, beef production, or aviation 'climate neutral', then the resources needed to account for the residual emissions left at the end of the greenhouse gas accounting sheet are likely to be used up before addressing them has even begun (McLaren et al., 2019; Carton et al., 2021).

Based on these developments, one could argue that geoengineering in the form of large-scale CDR has already become baked into the matter of contemporary climate politics. The Paris Agreement embraces it by defining action against climate change as a matter of achieving a 'balance between anthropogenic emissions by sources and removals by sinks of greenhouse gases'. The amount of negative emissions technologies in the IPCC's low-temperature pathways implies scales of CDR that are unprecedented, and – many argue – highly unrealistic. The enthusiasm of actors around the world in setting mid-century net zero targets that are distinctly vague about their reliance on carbon removal places additional pressure and expectations on the availability of resources needed. Although many modellers who rely on large-scale BECCS and afforestation to simulate low-temperature pathways vehemently argue against labelling this approach as 'geoengineering', there is no doubt that if realized, the scale of carbon removal currently projected would have profound global impacts the Earth's natural and social systems.

2.3 The Road to (Solar) Geoengineering

While negative emissions technologies and 'net zero' entered mainstream climate science via the integrated assessment modelling community, a different community of mostly US- (and later UK-based) researchers was exploring additional means of cooling the planet. Early front runners in this field, including scientists like David Keith (then of Carnegie Mellon University), Ken Caldeira, and Mike MacCracken (both of Lawrence Livermore National Laboratory) had already laid the foundations for a discussion on geoengineering in the 1990s (MacCracken, 1991; Keith and Dowlatabadi, 1992; Govindasamy and Caldeira, 2000). Importantly, their understanding of geoengineering included methods of both CDR and SRM.

As pessimism regarding the effectiveness of the Kyoto Protocol grew, their ideas found followers. The 2006 special issue in the journal *Climatic Change* with its editorial by Paul Crutzen reinforced the argument that geoengineering was worthy of scientific investigation, and this perception became reinforced by narratives of imminent crisis. An eyewitness from the time remembers the widespread discussion of new data from the US National Center for Atmospheric Research (NCAR) 'RAPID' programme, indicating the possible collapse of the Atlantic thermohaline circulation. The ensuing concern about a potential shutdown of Europe's primary source of warmth and other danger-ous tipping points led scientists in the United Kingdom to question the 'smooth projections of global change' that were seen to 'lull [society] into a sense of false security' (Lenton et al., 2008, p. 1792).[4] A common response to this narrative was that ensuring a stable climate would require a much more delib-erate approach to global climate management.

In reaction to a document published by the UK Royal Academy of Engineering, geoengineering was picked up by politicians in the United Kingdom. In March 2009, the UK House of Commons Committee on Innovation, Science and Skills (later renamed 'Science and Technology Committee') included the topic in a report on how the United Kingdom might improve its engineering capacity to remain internationally competitive (House of Commons, 2009). At the time, the Parliamentary Under-Secretary of State at the Department for Energy and Climate Change, Joan Ruddock, had expressed aversion to exploring geoengineering for two reasons. The first was that if 'Plan A' failed, there was little reason to imagine that 'Plan B' could succeed. The second was that investigating geoengineering could be interpreted as a reduction in commitment to mitigation or politically used in this way. Nevertheless, the committee remained enthusiastic about the potential for geoengineering and concluded that it would be 'negligent' to not consider geoengineering technologies as a Plan B, and that they should be evaluated as part of the portfolio of responses to climate change. It dismissed Ruddock's concerns as being a rehearsal of the arguments originally brought against adaptation, and were 'disappointed' that the government would revive such a 'discredited' argument (House of Commons, 2009, pp. 59–60).

---

[4] It was around this time that adaptation to climate change became more present on the international policy agenda, culminating in its equal footing with mitigation at the 2006 Bali COP. While the option had been recognized as existent during initial negotiations of the UNFCCC, its discussion had been discouraged in the United States due to fears that allowing for adaptation would endanger efforts at mitigation (Pielke *et al.*, 2007). The perceived process of taboo-lifting that adaptation went through was later an important reference for those advocating for research into geoengineering, who saw themselves facing a similar situation.

In April 2009, the UK committee members met with their counterpart in the United States, the Chairman of the Science and Technology Committee Bart Gordon. Gordon suggested that the two committees work together, and so they launched a collaborative investigation on geoengineering that included three congressional hearings in the United States and three oral panels in the United Kingdom (also see Schubert, 2021). Witnesses called upon during the US congressional hearings were mostly prominent geoengineering researchers, all of whom emphasized a need for establishing a comprehensive research programme. Among these, John Shepherd, David Keith, and Ken Caldeira also provided evidence for the UK investigation. Compared to the US committee however, the UK committee was more open to hearing experts from the wider field of climate research and policy. The effects of this can be seen in two resulting reports that summarize the investigations. While the UK report emphasizes a need to contextualize geoengineering in the wider landscape of environmental policy and identifies the United Nations as the forum through which any regulatory framework should eventually operate (House of Commons, 2010), the US report focuses the danger of stifling research endeavours through excessive regulation and emphasizes a need to support the generation of sound science on geoengineering (U.S. House of Representatives, 2010).

As these investigations were ongoing, Shepherd, Keith, and Caldeira, in collaboration with nine other scientists, published a report on the science, governance and uncertainty of geoengineering under the auspices of the UK Royal Society. The report's expressed aim was to 'provide an authoritative and balanced assessment of the main geoengineering options' in a subject area 'bedevilled by doubt and confusion' (Shepherd et al., 2009, p. v). In doing so, it delivered important input to the ongoing parliamentary hearings and endorsed the perspectives held by some of its more prominent co-authors. Importantly, it argued for a need to split geoengineering methods into CDR and SRM methods.[5] In this demarcation, CDR was considered largely benign and unproblematic, while SRM was described as being highly risky and in need of additional regulatory mechanisms. Each category included a wide range of possible technologies, ranging from land-use management to reflective shields in space.

---

[5] Steve Rayner, one of the two social scientists on the author list, later told me that this choice had been a point of contention. He had pointed out the political difficulties that such a categorization would lead to and suggested an alternative that divided technologies according to their degree of interference with the natural environment. He was outvoted by the natural scientists on the committee.

The framing of the Royal Society report had important effects on subsequent research and regulation. By defining geoengineering technologies according to chemical and physical process rather than scale, it nestled the controversial ideas that were generally thought of as geoengineering (stratospheric aerosol injection, ocean fertilization, or space mirrors) within a basket of many other, more familiar climate policy measures that were already used in local contexts. Later on, the distinction would contribute to deepening the divide between CDR and SRM researchers, as well as sow some amount of confusion amongst policymakers (Möller, 2020). It also initially directed the attention of geoengineering governance scholars to the group of technologies labelled as SRM, as these were portrayed as cheaper, more effective, but also more risky (Gupta and Möller, 2019).

The political attention dedicated to geoengineering and the publication of the Royal Society report acted as a kick-starter for expanding the research community. In March 2010, the philanthropy-backed Climate Response Fund financed a conference at which scientists, engineers and lawyers were invited to think about mechanisms that would ensure safe and responsible research into geoengineering techniques. Chaired by early geoengineering thought-leader Mike MacCracken, the conference was held at the Asilomar Centre in Monterey Bay, California, to mirror a famous earlier conference that had established voluntary guidelines on research of recombinant DNA. The scientific organizers aimed to produce a similar set of voluntary guidelines for geoengineering, although this did not quite pan out due to fundamental disagreements on definition and scope of what exactly should be governed.[6] Yet the conference had the effect of opening the field to more people and initiated a tradition of organizing workshops and conferences around the geoengineering theme, a process that, as I will explain in section 3, was key to eventually establishing geoengineering as a governance object.

Next to conferences and workshops, 2009–11 also saw a proliferation in research and outreach projects. In July 2009, the EU funded a three-year project called 'Implications and risks of engineering solar radiation management to limit climate change' (IMPLICC) to model the effectiveness and side effects of solar geoengineering. In March 2010, Andy Parker, who had co-authored the Royal Society report as a policy advisor, began directing the Solar Radiation

---

[6] At the time, many attendees were new to the concept and there was too much disagreement on what geoengineering actually was, whether carbon dioxide removal could be subsumed under the same umbrella as solar radiation management, and what acceptable outdoor research might look like, to collectively formulate a set of guidelines (Goodell, 2010). After several days of intense discussions, the organizing committee decided to recommend the adoption of an already existing set of principles (the so-called Oxford Principles (Rayner *et al.*, 2013), suggested by an ad hoc working group linked to the Royal Society report), although no formal endorsement of these principles took place.

Management Governance Initiative (SRMGI). Co-funded by the Royal Society, the Environmental Defense Fund and the World Academy of Sciences, SRMGI focuses on expanding the geoengineering governance conversation primarily by holding workshops in the Global South and providing funds for researchers in these countries to model the impacts of solar geoengineering on their own region (Kessler, 2019). Half a year later, two coordinated research projects were launched in the United Kingdom: the Integrated Assessment of Geoengineering Proposals and a sister project called 'Stratospheric Particle Injection for Climate Engineering' (SPICE). The initiative for these projects came from two of the most important public research councils in the United Kingdom, who aimed to 'fund research which will allow the United Kingdom to make intelligent and informed assessments about the development of Climate Geoengineering technologies' (Natural Environment Research Council, 2009). After evaluating strengths and blind-spots of the Royal Society report, the councils provided 4.5 and 3.5 years of funding respectively to establish multi-university, multi-disciplinary research ensembles that would evaluate natural, social, and technical aspects of geoengineering schemes. And finally, in 2011, a group of SRM modellers led by Ben Kravitz at Rutgers University started the Geoengineering Model Intercomparison Project (GeoMIP), a research community-run initiative to streamline the modelling of SRM and integrate its research into mainstream climate science.

In combination, these projects produced a surge of publications that brought the concept of 'geoengineering' to the attention of international climate science and policy. The sudden increase in scientific publications on geoengineering resulted in the first substantial treatment of geoengineering as a concept in the IPCC's 2013/2014 report (AR5). Its inclusion was extensively discussed during a two-day workshop in Lima, Peru, in June 2011. At this workshop, representatives from the three IPCC working groups met with prominent geoengineering experts (including David Keith and Ken Caldeira) to identify where and how the term geoengineering might feature in the report. A participant of the session illustratively described the meeting as being populated mainly by 'people who work exclusively or primarily on geoengineering', and that because 'when you're a hammer, everything is a nail', the attendants focused on identifying all the possible places where geoengineering might be integrated into the report. Much of the discussion revolved around how to best define geoengineering and how to ensure that geoengineering was included in a proportionate way. Eventually the authors suggested including the term geoengineering at the beginning of every working group report as well as in the synthesis report, and subsequently referring more specifically to CDR or SRM (Edenhofer et al., 2012).

To what degree the workshop informed the IPCC authors is unclear, but the geoengineering term did become a lot more prominent in the following AR5 report. Whereas earlier IPCC reports had mentioned geoengineering in passing, the physical science working group (WGI) of AR5 now dedicated a full paragraph to it at the end of its summary for policymakers. The paragraph was carefully worded and highlighted the limitations of both CDR and SRM, noting that 'CDR methods have biogeochemical and techno-logical limitations to their potential on a global scale' and that SRM methods 'have the potential to substantially offset a global temperature rise', but would also modify the global water cycle and not address ocean acidification (IPCC, 2013b, p. 29). It also spelled out that under its definition, large-scale BECCS, as used in the low-emissions scenarios of the earlier discussed RCP 2.6, was a form of geoengineering (IPCC, 2013a, p. 526). The mitigation working group (WG III) also dedicated several pages of text to discussing geoengineering techniques, with the authors noting that 'the literature on geoengineering options [...] has been increasing exponentially' (IPCC, 2014b, p. 125).

At this point there was already some amount of tension between the physical science group's and the mitigation group's understanding and use of the term. While the physical science group followed the Royal Society report's approach to defining geoengineering as 'the deliberate large-scale intervention in the Earth system to counter undesirable impacts of climate change' (IPCC, 2013a, p. 98) and dividing these interventions into CDR and SRM, the mitiga-tion working group (who had already been including BECCS in the earlier AR4 report) emphasized that geoengineering was a blanket term and that 'the boundary between some mitigation and some CDR methods is not always clear' (IPCC, 2014a, pp. 484, 1254). They also pointed out that that some studies considered afforestation and BECCS to be 'comparable with conven-tional mitigation methods' (IPCC, 2014a, p. 419).

As the mitigation group had relied heavily on large-scale BECCS and afforestation to model low-emissions pathways, they refrained from designat-ing these technologies as a form of geoengineering in their summary for policymakers. Only during the discussions of the mitigation working group plenary, in which countries had to approve the final wording of the summary for policymakers, did the topic arise. During the plenary, Bolivia's negotiator pointed out that the uncertainties and risks of relying on large-scale CDR were not sufficiently communicated, and that the use of 'geoengineering' and related options risked 'a new kind of invasion from developed countries' (Gutiérrez et al., 2014, p. 9). The resulting discussion ended in an agreement that the authors of the mitigation working group's summary for policymakers should refer to the biogeological and technological limitations of CDR that had been highlighted by the physical science working group (Petersen, 2014).

The IPCC's comparatively extensive engagement with geoengineering, based on its mandate to review the climate literature, came with further impetus and legitimization for the research field. Germany started its first large-scale coordinated research programme in 2013 under the title of 'SPP 1689 – Climate Engineering, Risks, Challenges, Opportunities', funded as a six-year priority programme under the German Research Council. China agreed to fund a researcher-initiated three-year programme on the modelling and governance of geoengineering technologies in 2015 under its National Basic Research Programme. And in the same year, the US National Academy of Sciences published the results of a government mandated inquiry resulting out of Bart Gordon's earlier investigation under the committee for science and technology (National Academy of Sciences, 2015).

By this time, geoengineering research had come to be seen as an acceptable scientific endeavour, even though most research projects still refrained from engaging in the development or testing of equipment for SRM technologies. (The earlier mentioned SPICE project in the United Kingdom had encountered some negative public attention around its test bed experiment and was likely seen as a warning to others in the field, see Cressey (2012).) The final confirmation of this perception came with the Paris Agreement in December 2015. At the time, I was attending the Earth System Governance conference in Canberra, and distinctly remember the celebrations held in the plenary session. The surprise announcement that countries had committed to a temperature target well below 2°C was met with much enthusiasm by all attendees. But for some of the attending scholars, it also raised concerns that such ambitious temperature targets would further justify research and development of large-scale CDR and SRM.

2.4 Contesting Geoengineering

As the scientific engagement with geoengineering grew, so did the concern that research would remain ungoverned. Over the course of 2014 and 2015, Hermann Graf von Hatzfeldt, a member of the German landed gentry, organized a series of retreats at his castle in the forests of western Germany. The retreats often took place without a dedicated agenda, inviting participants from European and American foundations to identify and discuss sustainability related issues that merited philanthropic support and attention. One of these meetings was dedicated to the topic of geoengineering. It included Irene Krarup, the executive director of the New York-based V. Kann Rasmussen Foundation, a philanthropy established by the founder of the Danish window company Velux. The geoengineering topic struck a chord of concern with the foundation, and in Autumn 2016, Krarup approached the German Heinrich Böll Foundation to announce her intentions of supporting civil society action to ensure that proper regulation for this topic would come to pass. The idea was to create an organization that would conduct back-door diplomacy, lobbying policymakers behind the scenes to ensure that proper regulation for geoengineering research and development was put in place.

From this idea resulted the birth of the Carnegie Climate Geoengineering Governance initiative, widely known as C2G2. In 2017, Janos Pasztor, a Hungarian Diplomat who had formerly worked for the United Nations and the Worldwide Fund for Nature, was employed to establish and run the organization. But Krarup also thought that if governments would start talking about geoengineering, it would need a strong civil society to contribute to the debate. The V. Kann Rasmussen Foundation therefore offered additional funding to three civil society advocacy organizations – the Heinrich Böll Foundation, the ETC Group, and the Climate Action Network – to act as watchdogs over the unfolding geoengineering policy discussion.

Both the Heinrich Böll Foundation and the ETC Group had been vocal critics of geoengineering research since many years. Together with Greenpeace and the International Union for Conservation of Nature, the ETC Group had led the 2007 campaign against ocean iron fertilization that resulted in regulation on marine geoengineering under the London Convention on Marine Pollution. The Heinrich Böll Foundation later supported the ETC Group in writing their 'Geopiracy' report, warning of risks related to scientific advancement in the field and calling for a moratorium on real-world experimentation (ETC Group, 2010).

The ETC Group and the Heinrich Böll Foundation continued their activities in raising awareness and mobilizing civil society networks, but also by giving input to the newly created C2G2 initiative for which ETC initially sat on the advisory panel. Yet as time progressed, it became clear that the interests and perspectives of the organizations were diverging. While ETC and the Böll Foundation maintained their highly critical perspective on geoengineering, C2G2's more neutral approach to expanding the conversation on geoengineering governance without taking an explicit critical position was perceived by the NGOs as a form of lobbying for the technologies themselves. Relations between C2G2 and the two advocacy organizations deteriorated, and eventually, ETC left the advisory panel. The watchdog organizations continued their work in collaboration with more critical civil society partners, teaming up with organizations like the Center for International Environmental Law, the Indigenous

Environmental Network, Biofuelwatch, and the Global Forest Coalition. Under the auspices of their 'Hands Off Mother Earth' (HOME) campaign and their online presence, the 'Geoengineering Monitor', they built an international network of advocacy organizations that tracked developments in geoengineering research, provided critical information to both governments and the wider public, and mobilized resistance to outdoor research and experimentation around the world.

In the meantime, the scientific conversation around geoengineering had shifted and a diversity of new vocabulary was proposed to describe some of the approaches that had formerly been subsumed under geoengineering (also see Boettcher, 2020). The 2015 report by the National Academy of Sciences started using the term 'climate intervention', and chose to replace the term SRM with 'albedo modification' or 'reflecting sunlight' (McNutt et al., 2015). In reaction to the proliferation of carbon removal strategies in mainstream climate models, NGOs were seeking for a way to distinguish between technological and ecosystem-based approaches and introduced the term 'nature-based solutions' (Cohen-Sacham et al., 2016). The IPCC explicitly stopped using the term geoengineering in its 2018 special report on 1.5°C, instead placing CDR (now using the IAM vocabulary of 'negative emissions technologies') in the same basket with 'other mitigation options' and keeping SRM (now termed 'solar radiation modification') separate (de Coninck et al., 2018). The United Kingdom supported research into large-scale CDR under the term 'Greenhouse Gas Removal' (Climate Change Committee, 2019). And in June 2019, C2G2 removed the word geoengineering from its name, renaming itself as 'the Carnegie Climate Governance Initiative' (C2G).

It looked like across the board, actors were distancing themselves from the word geoengineering and finding more technical or benign terminology with less controversial connotation. Only a few actors continued using it. These included those who had criticized it for many years, and those who had advocated for placing it on the research agenda in the first place. Thus, the ETC Group and the Heinrich Böll Foundation continued their activities under the banner of the 'Geoengineering Monitor', and the still ongoing GeoMIP modelling project and a research programme at Harvard co-directed by Professors David Keith and Frank Keutsch started using the term 'solar geoengineering' in 2017 to describe SRM technologies. Harvard continued using this term in their programme title and consistently referred to it in subsequent publications, even after the IPCC abandoned the term 'geoengineering' entirely.

While a large part of academia was occupied with debating and adjusting terminology, policymakers went ahead in an effort to address geoengineering under the United Nations for a second time. On 4 March 2019, the Swiss delegation to the United Nations Environment Assembly tabled a draft for a resolution to explore the possibility of regulating geoengineering. Supported by a diverse set of countries, the draft called on the Executive Director of the United Nations Environment Programme to prepare an assessment of geoengineering technologies and their governance implications.[7] In its preamble, the text expressed a deep concern about the potential risks and adverse effects of geoengineering the environment. It welcomed ongoing work in other international bodies, recognizing the work of the IPCC, the Convention on Biological Diversity and the London Convention, but also noted the mandate of the United Nations Environment Programme to keep an eye on emerging environmental issues of international significance.

The UNEA resolution proposal was worded in neutral language, did not spell out any kind of regulation, and was deemed open and welcoming by commentators beforehand – even those sympathetic to geoengineering research (McLaren and Corry, 2021a). Nevertheless, it met substantial push back. According to a civil society observant of the negotiations at the summit, most countries were not aware that the topic was being discussed, and therefore negotiations took place between a smaller set of parties. Supporting the proposal were Switzerland and the countries that had signed the proposal; the European Union, who was well prepared because of Germany's active engagement with the topic; and Bolivia, as their negotiator had formerly dealt with geoengineering under the Convention on Biological Diversity. Countering the resolution were the United States and Saudi Arabia, who vehemently opposed any action under the UN Environment Assembly. They argued that addressing geoengineering in this context risked veering into the political domain of climate change and the mandate of the IPCC – a memorable move, considering that the United States under President Trump and Saudi Arabia were not otherwise known for defending the work of the IPCC or the functionality of the climate change regime in general. Further efforts by proponents to find a consensus in changing the assessment into a report and requiring cooperation with other international bodies were futile, and so Switzerland withdrew the resolution on 13 March (Earth Negotiations Bulletin, 2019).

Behind the scenes, (solar) geoengineering was also popping up in other places. One of these places was the International Organization for Standardization, widely abbreviated as ISO. The ISO is a non-governmental organization that publishes worldwide technical, industrial, and commercial

---

[7] Countries supporting the Swiss resolution were Burkina Faso, Micronesia, Georgia, Lichtenstein, Mali, Mexico, Montenegro, New Zealand, Niger, South Korea, and Senegal. Many of these collaborate in global climate negotiations as the so-called Environmental Integrity Group (Ingold and Pflieger, 2016).

standards, ranging from camera film speed to anti-bribery management systems. In late 2018, it accepted a new work item proposal titled 'Radiative Forcing Management – Guidance for the quantification and reporting of radiative forcing-based climate footprints and mitigation efforts'. The proposal was initiated by two US environmental certification companies, and justified as a guide for private organizations to quantify their climate footprint by accounting for short lived climate pollutants such as aerosols, methane, or soot. As a part of its standardization measures, it proposed the creation of so-called radiative forcing credits that could be traded on an international market. What this meant was that companies could estimate their ultimate impact on the climate by balancing warming and cooling effects. The reflectivity of soot or sulphur dioxide emissions would then become creditable as a counterbalance to the warming effect of carbon dioxide emissions. Particularly for large emitters like the shipping or airline industry (who in the short term contribute to global cooling through condensation trails caused be emissions of particulate matter), this would probably have been a welcome initiative.

The proposal, titled 'ISO 14082', met significant resistance in the international working group dedicated to its negotiation, which consisted of experts from the United States, Australia, Austria, Canada, Germany, and later Norway and Malaysia (Seifert and Bräker, 2020). Main points of contention were that the balance of radiative forcing was not well understood yet from a scientific point of view, and that a standard like this would incentivize cooling projects through aerosol emissions instead of maintaining the focus on greenhouse gas emissions reductions established under Kyoto. Although ISO standards are voluntary, they are widely accepted and used to execute international law, for example, Article 6 of the Paris Agreement on carbon markets. The negotiations became so intense that their time frame was extended from twenty-four to thirty-six months. Eventually, the opponents succeeded in demoting the standard to the status of a technical report, although discussions around its wording carried on well into the summer of 2021.

Another place where solar geoengineering appeared unexpectedly was Sweden. In December 2020, the Harvard Solar Geoengineering Research Program announced that it would collaborate with the Swedish Space Corporation in Kiruna to launch a 600 kg package of scientific equipment into the stratosphere via a space balloon as a part of their 'Stratospheric Controlled Perturbation Experiment' (SCoPEx). Scheduled for June 2021, the purpose of the launch was to test manoeuvring and communications equipment in preparation for further experiments to study the release of small amounts of reflective particles (Doyle, 2020). The announcement that the launch would take place in Sweden came as a surprise to many. The Harvard researchers had made earlier plans to conduct outdoor experiments at space stations in the United States, the most recent of which was to launch a balloon in Arizona using the services of a private aeronautic company. But in a letter to the experiment's advisory panel, the project leader Frank Keutsch explained that they would collaborate with the Swedish Space Corporation instead, as contract issues, Covid-19, and other logistical challenges made it impossible to arrange an experiment in the United States for the desired time frame (Keutsch, 2020).

Shortly after the December 15 announcement to proceed with the SCoPEx experiment, the civil society watchdog NGOs and their Geoengineering Monitor published a statement that criticized the experiment and called on 'all people's and social movements and organizations that work with a climate justice agenda to be on alert to stop SCoPEx, including the proposed experiments in Sweden' (Geoengineering Monitor, 2021). Over the course of the next months, widely circulated Swedish newspapers published a row of critical articles about the experiment. They included an op-ed by fossil fuel divestment activist Bill McKibben in *Dagens Nyheter*, warning that the experiment would endanger the global momentum on climate action that was finally taking shape (McKibben, 2021); and an op-ed by the deputy director of the Stockholm Resilience Center Victor Galaz in *Svenska Dagbladet*, calling the 'political naivety' with which the Swedish Space Corporation had decided to collaborate on this experiment 'remarkable' (Galaz, 2021).

In the meantime, the Indigenous community of Northern Europe represented by the Saami Council and several Swedish environmental organizations sent an open letter to the SCoPEx advisory board, asking them to cancel the test flight. Copying in the Swedish Space Corporation and the Swedish Government, they noted that the project had at no time consulted with Swedish authorities; that its advisory board did not include any representatives from the country hosting the experiment; and that they found the project's approach to ethics, responsibility and decision-making problematic as it refused to engage with larger questions of stratospheric aerosol injection governance (Saami Council, 2021). The public pressure created by media and non-state actors during February and March 2021 resulted in a withdrawal of the project. On 31 March, the Swedish Space Corporation announced that the test flight would not be conducted that summer, with the SCoPEx advisory committee adding that any test flights would need to be suspended until robust and inclusive public engagement had occurred. In reaction to the decision, David Keith said he 'doubted that anyone knew how widespread opposition was in Sweden', citing public engagement surveys that showed support for such experiments (Fountain and Flavelle, 2021).

As I am writing these lines, the most recent contestation of geoengineering is manifesting itself. In January 2022, a coalition of predominantly governance and political science scholars published an open letter to propose an international non-use agreement for solar geoengineering. In motivating their call, they argue that any democratic governance of a global intervention like stratospheric aerosol injection would be impossible in the existing political context (Biermann et al., 2022). The letter was widely picked up and engaged with by different national media, and received scorching criticism from scientists engaging with solar geoengineering research, in particular through the medium of Twitter. Some reactions included accusations of being 'illiberal', 'undemocratic', and incompatible with an 'enlightenment framework', some even questioning the legitimacy, seniority, and expertise of the initiative's proponents (see the 'Solar Geoengineering Non-Use Agreement' Twitter thread). Observers in the field express different opinions about the merits of proposing such a non-use agreement, but the initiative shows that 'geoengineering' as a concept is (still) perceived to be a distinct and salient governance object. Interestingly however, the divorce of CDR and SRM, supported by the activities of integrated assessment modellers and the IPCC, has directed most contestation efforts towards SRM. We can thus conclude that at least part of the concept (notably everything that can be associated with CDR), has transformed into a more malleable version that is increasingly being integrated into mainstream climate policy.

So what does all of this tell us about why geoengineering emerged on the global scientific and political agenda? Following the account in this section, we can understand geoengineering as a result of activities in the realms of climate politics, science, and advocacy. In it, we see actors engaging with geoengineering in different ways – some of them legitimizing it as an important Plan B in the face of climate crisis, others discrediting it as a dangerous form of hubris and distraction, and yet others trying to distance themselves entirely from the concept while maintaining some of its fundamental ideas. What is important to note here is that geoengineering as a governance object evolved at the intersection of these different communities, and that in their interaction, these communities contributed to shaping geoengineering as a distinct, salient and, at least partly, malleable governance object. To better understand how this co-creation between communities took place, let us now take a closer look at the social dynamics that characterize this interaction.

3 The Geoengineering Knowledge Network

Beyond tracing conceptual origins, I argue that explaining the emergence of geoengineering as a governance object also requires understanding the network of people who gathered around and interacted with the idea. In the wider geoengineering literature, the core of this network often appears as the so-called 'Geoclique', a term coined by *Science* magazine reporter Eli Kintisch (2010) that embodies the subjective experience of many observers that there is, indeed, a distinct, narrow, and influential community of people linked to the geoengineering concept. This community has been described by critics as being key to shaping important debates in the field, including the normalization of ideas to deliberately control the climate, the mobilization of funding to support their research endeavours, and the propagation of a 'Panglossian' (i.e., excessively optimistic) view on international politics (Porter and Hulme, 2013; Anshelm and Hansson, 2014a; McKinnon, 2019).

Yet given the previous exploration of the geoengineering trajectory, I argue that looking exclusively at this core community does not cover the full story. In this section, I try to understand how the social dynamics within the core community and in its engagement with rivalling communities in the wider knowledge network contributed to turning geoengineering into a governance object. My approach here is to first quantitatively map the geoengineering core community and then qualitatively explore its interaction with other communities. To support this, I use three conceptual tools from social network analysis. These include the concept of 'social cohesion', meaning the willingness of members to be part of a community (Friedkin, 2004); the concept of 'brokerage', meaning the potential of some actors to shape the content of a network's discourse by bridging different groups (Burt, 2005); and the concept of 'network diversity' or 'weak ties', a proxy indicator for the adaptability of a network through information diffusion and innovation (Granovetter, 1973).

From a theoretical point of view, I argue that social cohesion, brokerage, and diversity can be directly linked to the three characteristics that Olaf Corry (2013) identifies as necessary for a governance object to gain traction: distinctiveness, saliency, and malleability. In combination, they describe a set of mechanisms that help explain how knowledge networks produce governance objects (see Box 2). The three mechanisms should be thought of as interdependent and overlapping processes, although the fact that an idea must begin in a smaller group before it can expand suggests that there is some temporal ordering to their prominence. The advantage of these three mechanisms is that they can be used in both a quantitative and a qualitative setting. They provide measurable indicators to identify and compare different knowledge networks, as well as a theoretical lens through which to qualitatively study the social interactions and activities within a knowledge network.

To quantitatively map the geoengineering core community, I used the programmes of geoengineering workshops and conferences, reasoning that those

BOX 2 LINKING KNOWLEDGE NETWORKS TO GOVERNANCE OBJECTS

Social cohesion is defined as the individual group members' attitudes and behaviours towards the group, notably their desire to belong and their degree of participation. Here, the existence of social cohesion is understood as a prerequisite for a community's existence, while simultaneously explaining its members tendency to conform to common behavioural norms and converge on a set of ideas that create a distinct governance object. Cohesion is particularly important in the beginning, when the community establishes itself around a given object and needs to make that object distinct in order to create a shared identity.

Brokerage is defined as the capacity of individuals to bridge so-called structural holes in a network. People who form links between otherwise unconnected groups often take on entrepreneurial or opinion-forming roles. The reason for their success becomes understandable when considering the need to create compatibility with existing norms and ideas – an indicator for the success of a knowledge network. Here, brokerage is used to explain the evolution of salience in a governance object. Brokerage can be thought of as important in the initial expansion of the community, where targeted framing is needed to make the community and its governance object attractive (or 'salient') for new members to engage with.

Network diversity is here defined as the variety of societal realms, organizations, and disciplines represented in a knowledge network. My use of it is inspired by an influential sociological theory about the 'strength of weak ties', which states that information travels quicker and better in a network that contains many acquaintances ('weak ties') than in a network that is full of close friends ('strong ties'). Diversity is the latest step in the process and can be conceptualized as a self-reinforcing outcome of successful brokerage. In theory, a salient object that attracts engagement by different communities will result in a more diverse network, which in turn spreads information and leads to even more diversity, contestation, and deliberation. Contestation and deliberation, in turn, is what makes the object malleable and applicable in many different contexts.

who make the effort to repeatedly attend and present at such events demonstrate significant dedication to the group. The events were identified through the archives of the 'geoengineering google group', a news server that distributes updates about discussions, blogs, publications and events related to geoengineering. My main criterion for inclusion was the independence of the event (panels within larger conferences were not included), and an explicit reference to geoengineering or its sub-technologies in the title.[8]

In total, I identified ninety geoengineering related events that took place between 2006 and 2018. Out of these, I had access to the programme in seventy-four cases, resulting in a database of 1,080 individual speaking participants. I then divided the database into two temporal phases: an 'early' network (thirty-five events between 2006 and 2013) and a 'late' network (thirty-nine events between 2014 and 2018). Splitting the analysis into two phases made it somewhat easier to interpret the resulting networks and see changes in the network structure. The split is approximately contemporary with the publication of the 2013/2014 fifth integrated assessment report of the IPCC, an event associated with a qualitative change in the geoengineering discussion and network (see Section 2). I then mapped networks showing both events and members in each phase, including only those speakers who had attended a minimum of two events in the given time frame. Brokerage and diversity within the core community were subsequently assessed by calculating the total amount of shortest paths leading through a given individual ('betweenness centrality') and by coding for the network members' disciplinary background, organizational realm and whether they were male or female.[9]

3.1 The Invisible College

The first step in this analysis is to explore the relationship between the social cohesion of the network and the distinctiveness of geoengineering as a governance object. Using network analysis, I identified a group of about 100 individuals who were actively engaged in the two phases of the geoengineering discussion (2006–13 and 2014–18). This points to the existence of a core community in which members regularly met at conferences and workshops, and resonates with findings in the literature on so-called invisible colleges (Price, 1983). Invisible colleges are described as informal communication networks of approximately 100 elite scholars from different affiliations who confer power and prestige to one another through citations, co-authorship and common projects (Zuccala, 2006). While there are different ways of mapping them, the main characteristics that define invisible colleges are that they work on the same issue (clustered around different sub-categories), that they collaborate to gain

---

[8] This included geoengineering, climate engineering, climate intervention, climate modification, solar radiation management, carbon dioxide/greenhouse gas removal, direct air capture, BECCS, and negative (carbon) emissions technology.

[9] 'Betweenness centrality' is a measure that describes the brokerage potential of an individual in a network and an indicator for the ability to frame information to new audiences (Freeman, 1979). It captures the idea that in order for one network member to reach any other network member, there is a 'shortest path' that they can follow. If a certain person happens to lie on many of these shortest paths, then they are attributed a high level of betweenness centrality.

funding, and that they find means and ways to meet regularly – for example, through workshops and conferences.

Figures 1a and b show graphs of the geoengineering core community in two temporal phases, depicting the events and the individuals who attended at least two events in a given period. The colour-coding of the events reveals that before

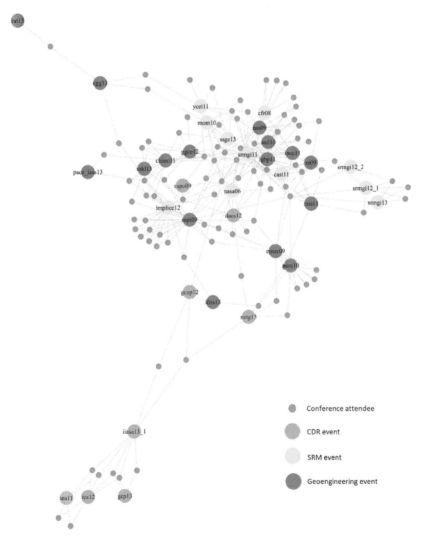

Figure 1a Conferences and workshops organized during the early (2006–13) phase of the geoengineering knowledge network. Red nodes indicate individuals who participated as speakers at more than one event and are therefore considered part of the geoengineering core community.
Source: Author's compilation

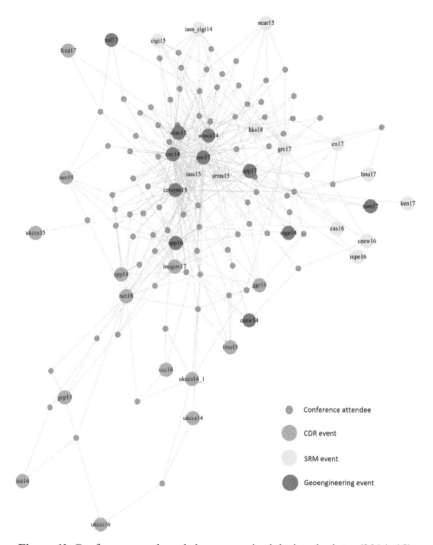

Figure 1b Conferences and workshops organised during the later (2014–18) phase of the geoengineering knowledge network.

2013, those attending events on SRM and geoengineering in general (GE) were one well integrated group, with only few who also attended events dedicated to CDR. By contrast, the core community after 2013 indicates much more activity in the field of CDR, an increasing split towards either attending events on CDR or SRM, and less activity under the geoengineering umbrella term. Nevertheless, the umbrella term events still serve as a way of 'gluing' the two parts of the core community together, a role that is much less pronounced in the earlier phase of the network.

Qualitative analysis reveals the story of a somewhat involuntary marriage between rivalling communities that took place in the wake of the IPCC's fifth assessment report. Before this marriage, we can trace the development of two largely separate communities of Earth systems scientists: one evolving out of the narrative to consider geoengineering technologies to complement conventional climate policy (the geoengineering community – see Section 2.3), and one evolving out of the narrative to use biological and terrestrial sinks for climate risk management (the IAM community) (see Section 2.2).

Both communities had the goal to provide an affordable backstop solution in the face of uncertainties associated with climate change. Yet the two communities operated largely independent of each other until 2014, when it became apparent that almost all low-temperature scenarios in IPCC's fifth assessment report relied on massive amounts of BECCS to stay below 2°C. Because few people outside the IAM community had previously been aware of this, this community was suddenly confronted with the same types of problems and critiques that the geoengineering community had been confronted with: desirability, moral hazard, and a slippery slope scenario through technological lock-in. The result of this critique, and the need for alternatives to BECCS in order to invoke the massive drawdown of CO_2 proposed in the models, resulted in a merging of communities, with more members of the geoengineering core community also becoming part of the IAM community.

The initially parallel operation of these two communities, despite their common goal, indicates the existence of initially distinct governance objects. Early publications that herald the initiation of the two communities outline their constitutional narratives. In one of the first seminal papers on geoengineering, David Keith (2000) defined geoengineering as a third, remedial measure that is different from mitigation and adaptation, and that can be separated into methods which either remove carbon from the atmosphere, or that reflect incoming sunlight. He argued that geoengineering research is necessary because of its potential to act as a backstop for mitigation failure, and because ignoring it might lead to large-scale human intervention without the necessary critical and ethical evaluation.[10] This framing of geoengineering and the need to conduct research on it has since been found to constitute an overarching argumentation pattern of researchers who gravitate towards the geoengineering concept (Anshelm and Hansson, 2014b).

---

[10] Keith's particular concern was that greenhouse gas removal through biological sinks was being divorced from more 'objectionable' technologies, indicating a move towards the acceptance of geoengineering-like proposals without conducting a proper debate about ethics. This early concern reflects a critique of the community that was to evolve around BECCS and carbon sinks, which did not consider its work a form of geoengineering (Obersteiner *et al.*, 2001).

Meanwhile, early publications in the IAM community defined 'Biomass Energy Carbon Sequestration' (BECS) as a technology that is *different* from geoengineering based on variations in uncertainty and risk (Obersteiner, 2001). Because terrestrial CDR is considered well understood, the authors defined it as form of necessary, urgent, and largely unproblematic mitigation. They argued that research is needed because the uncertainties of climate modelling and political decision-making necessitate investment in a risk-hedging technology. Their basic justification is thus similar to the lead narratives that also motivate the geoengineering community. It is their strong emphasis that terrestrial CDR is safe mitigation and *not* dangerous geoengineering that served as a key reason for forming an entirely different community, and that persists in contemporary literature produced by its members.

How does social cohesion then contribute to creating a distinct governance object? Important here are social mechanisms of creating and maintaining order that lead new community members to adhere to original language and problem definitions. One way in which this seems to happen is through narratives of common cause. Attendees of early geoengineering conferences explained to me that when facing criticism from outside, members of the early geoengineering community would reason that geoengineering was comparable to adaptation, and that while adaptation once used to be the 'poor cousin' of mitigation, it was eventually placed on equal footing and is now rightly recognized as an important part of climate policy. It was therefore worth engaging in the common cause of addressing controversial issues like geoengineering despite scepticism from other groups. Such narratives created a feeling of togetherness, incentivizing new members to engage in the community's projects and activities, and to adopt the community's language and its basic assumptions.

Another mechanism ensuring internal cohesion seems to be social control. At some of the conferences I attended, it was clear that those who openly criticized the community's cause could expect harsh reactions. Some scholars who fundamentally questioned the value of engaging with geoengineering told me they perceived the research environment as 'acrimonious' or 'hostile', sometimes creating enough pressure for them to withdraw from the field after a few years of engagement. This could happen through dedicated ignoring of fundamental critique or public questioning of the critic's legitimacy. Social mechanisms of maintaining order within the community thus also seem to have played a role in creating and upholding a distinct language and conceptualization of geoengineering in the early phase of the network.

Yet, social cohesion is not only relevant within the geoengineering core community. It is also relevant in the rivalling communities that it engages with. For example, the network of critical civil society organizations discussed in Section 2.4 no doubt played an equally important role in making geoengineering a distinctive governance object. In targeting their critique, they themselves are dependent on sharing and maintaining a stable object that can carry their narrative of danger and hubris. Through websites like the 'Geoengineering Monitor' or the 'HOME campaign', these advocacy organizations reproduce geoengineering as a separate and relevant object of governance. By pointing out projects, experiments and initiatives that they consider to be evidence of 'geoengineering', they maintain the concept's distinctiveness and fill it with content that establishes geoengineering as a real and salient object of concern.

3.2 Knowledge Brokers and Attraction Narratives

The second step in this analysis is to explore the relationship between the brokerage potential of the network and the salience of geoengineering as a governance object. Figure 2 shows a collapsed version of the geoengineering core community, in which the events are removed and individuals share ties based on having attended at least two events together. The size of each node is proportional to the node's betweenness centrality measure.[11] We can see that in the early phase of the network, brokerage potential is concentrated amongst a few individuals. Many of these names will be familiar to those who study the geoengineering literature. Their high level of betweenness centrality can be attributed to bridging different sub-clusters of the community. For example, David Keith of Harvard University is a central figure in bridging research groups in the United Kingdom and United States and research groups in the EU. Similarly, Andy Parker, having been a fellow both at Harvard and the IASS, bridges these two groups and additionally provides the principal connection to researchers from non-Western countries through the SRMGI. Finally, Henrik Karlsson, one of the earliest entrepreneurs in the field of BECCS and CEO of the Swedish start-up company 'Bioecro', acted as an early broker between the geoengineering and the IAM community.

Qualitative investigations provide insights to the function of such brokers in the core community. Interviewees whom I asked about how they first connected with the geoengineering topic tended to speak of an event at which they witnessed a prominent leader of the discussion (often overlapping with one the brokerage figures in Figure 2a), and their most salient message. The saliency and memorability of the brokers' main messages indicates their use of what

---

[11] As a reminder: the betweenness centrality measure gives the total amount of shortest paths between any two nodes that lead through a single individual, providing an indicator for the individuals ability to frame information to new audiences.

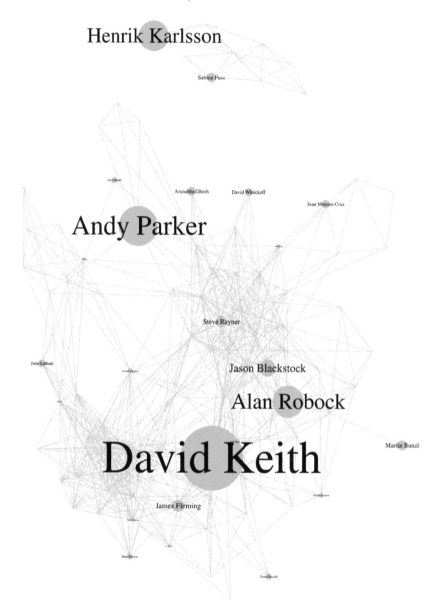

Figure 2a Knowledge brokers in the early (2006–13) phase of the geoengineering knowledge network. Nodes are sized according to their betweenness centrality, indicating their potential to shape information and importance in holding the network together.

Source: Author's compilation

John Moore

Sabine Fuss

Andreas Oschlies

Janos Pasztor

Oliver Geden

Stefan Schaefer

David Keith

Jessica Strefler

David Keller

Simon Nicholson

Duncan McLaren

Andrew Lockley

Tim Kruger

Joshua Horton

Anna-Maria Hubert

Jane Flegal

Oliver Morton

Thomas Ackerman

Phil Rasch

Olivier Boucher

Figure 2b Knowledge brokers in the later (2014–2018) phase of the geoengineering knowledge network.

might be called 'attraction narratives'. These narratives were usually expressed in a simple graph or chart that depicted an immediate urgency (the problem), or the low cost and simplicity of the object in question (the solution). One example was provided by an Earth system scientist who recalled her engagement in the early phases of the geoengineering knowledge network. She explained that a key figure shown at conferences demonstrated how current greenhouse gas emissions were higher than any scenarios calculated by the IPCC, often combined with incoming data about the suspected breakdown of the thermohaline circulation. Another interviewee stated how geoengineering, in particular stratospheric aerosol injection, was subsequently presented as the solution. In back-of-the-envelope calculations, it was shown to be a cheap, fast, and simple backstop measure to address an imminent climate emergency. Between 2006–9, these images and narratives served as powerful reasons begin engaging with geoengineering and explain why SRM in particular became an early, salient object for the geoengineering core community.

In the later version of the network (Figure 2b), the potential to shape discourses through brokering is much less concentrated, although there seems to be a new niche for brokerage in bridging the original geoengineering core community with its newcomers. Many of these brokers are well-known social scientists in the geoengineering literature, including Anna-Maria Hubert, Duncan McLaren, Tim Kruger, Stefan Schaefer, and Joshua Horton. We also see the emergence of brokers like Sabine Fuss and David Keller, scientists who work exclusively with CDR. This increased distribution and diversity of brokerage potential heralds engagement with more critical, governance and ethics-oriented perspectives on geoengineering. It also goes hand in hand with a questioning of basic concepts and assumptions that had previously served as foundational narratives in the geoengineering core community. Most prominently, the terms 'negative emissions technologies' and 'greenhouse gas removal' were now introduced as alternative concepts to the original CDR term. Also the term 'geoengineering' itself was experiencing more confrontation, with members of the IAM community challenging the grouping of carbon removal and SRM under one umbrella term.

Interviews and observations indicate that attraction narratives in this later network revolved more strongly around CDR. One important narrative often used by prominent knowledge brokers in the IAM community is about the limited feasibility of so-called deep-mitigation scenarios demanded by policymakers. It is usually enforced through graphs that show extremely steep emissions reductions if the 1.5°C is to be reached by 2100. The offered solution is consequently presented with a flattening of these graphs if negative emissions technologies are added to conventional mitigation measures (see Fuss et al., 2020). In the IAM community, BECCS has traditionally played a prominent role in this solution narrative, the argument being that bioenergy and CCS are two already well-known technologies that could rapidly be deployed at large scale. When the 2015 Paris Agreement explicitly included 1.5°C as a long-term global goal, the narrative became particularly powerful, explaining some of the recent increase in saliency of CDR.

Brokers and attraction narratives did not only contribute to enhancing salience within the core community; they also did so outside. Knowledge brokers in the previously discussed community of advocacy organizations played a key role in transporting their highly critical message about geoengineering to a much wider network of political and civil society organizations. By organizing strategic meetings around geoengineering conferences and engaging with civil society actors at large climate events (such as the 2018 Global Climate Action Summit in California), knowledge brokers from within organizations like the Heinrich Böll Foundation and the ETC Group could involve and mobilize other organizations and networks who were sympathetic to their cause. Also by being in contact with and providing advice to policymakers, both nationally and internationally, these knowledge brokers helped define geoengineering as an important and salient governance object in need of political attention.

3.3 Mix and Match

The third step in this analysis is to explore the relationship between the diversity of the knowledge network and the malleability of a governance object. Figure 3 demonstrates that the geoengineering core community is quite diverse in some ways, and very homogeneous in others. Despite being an object born of the Earth system sciences, the knowledge network that gathered around it includes a significant amount of professionals from the social sciences and humanities. Political science, economics, law, and philosophy make-up approximately 25 per cent of the core network; atmospheric science and geoscience make-up approximately 30 per cent. In terms of organizational diversity, the geoengineering core community consists primarily of individuals from research institutions and think tanks, but also demonstrates connections to organizations outside the research sector. These connections are built primarily by individuals who span different realms, most of them having an affiliation in both research and civil society, government or the private sector. By contrast, the distribution between men and women is very much skewed in one direction, with men making up 88 per cent of the early core network and 81 per cent of the later core network.

Diversity of disciplines in the geoengineering core community seems to have served as a motor for incremental adaptation of the geoengineering concept and developed it in a way that made it interesting to a wider audience. Observations and document analysis show that as members of different disciplines regularly meet at workshops and conferences, they highlight to each other how

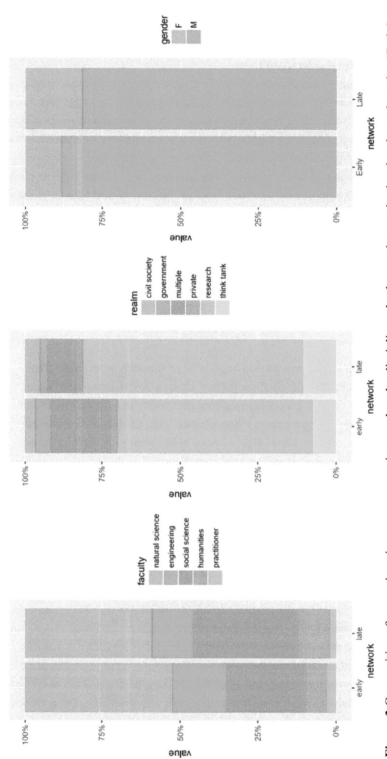

Figure 3 Composition of geoengineering core community members by disciplinary background, organizational realm and gender. 'Early' refers to the period 2006–13, 'late' refers to the period 2014–18.

Source: Author's compilation

geoengineering is an object of interest in many different contexts. These interdisciplinary discussions result in physicists discussing questions of equity and philosophers discussing alterations in rainfall, and at some point, all members of the community know exactly how the concept relates to a whole range of different concerns. As a result, they are also able to present geoengineering in a nuanced but cohesive manner to interested observers, including policymakers. Particularly in the case of stratospheric aerosol injection, deliberation and contextualization across disciplines has adapted and changed the technology from a wild idea to save the planet, into a serious object of research deemed worthy of further investigation and in need of adequate governance.

Diversity in organizational background seems to have served as a motor for diffusion of the geoengineering concept. Through connections with governments, NGOs and the private sector, geoengineering travelled from a purely scholarly context into other societal arenas. Once it arrived on the agenda of non-academic actors, the members of the community (most often its opinion shaping brokers) were asked to provide further evidence and information on the subject, reinforcing whatever discourse the community upheld in the outside world. Examples include the earlier discussed meeting of the IPCC in Peru, where members of the geoengineering core community advised IPCC authors on how geoengineering might be addressed in its fifth assessment report (Edenhofer et al., 2012); members' participation in writing the CBD's report on geoengineering; or members serving as witnesses for US congress hearings on the subject. In this way, organizational diversity helped spread the concept into political realms, creating the impression that geoengineering was indeed an important and widely discussed issue.

By contrast, the imbalance between male and female network members confirms findings about male dominance in the geoengineering debate and reflects the under-representation of female voices in public media and scientific literature on the topic (Buck et al., 2014; Stephens and Surprise, 2020). It also adds to findings that show an under-representation of researchers and perspectives from the Global South in the geoengineering knowledge network (Biermann and Möller, 2019). The most important concern related to this over-representation of Western male perspectives is that it can lead to a so-called white male effect, where benefits become overestimated and risks become more tolerated. According to this theory, white men are generally more privileged and experience less exposure to environmental hazards and side effects of technological innovation (Flynn et al., 1994). It is possible that such an over-representation of Western men in the geoengineering knowledge network may have contributed to creating a narrative where geoengineering techniques are perceived as feasible and desirable solutions to the problem of climate change, and where the benefits of research and development outweigh its risks.

While disciplinary and organizational diversity within the network led to incremental adaptation, larger changes in the community's discourse seemed to happen only through engagement with rival communities. After the IPCC's fifth assessment report, the IAM community was forced to engage with allegations of geoengineering through massive use of BECCS in their 2°C models. But members of the IAM community have traditionally distinguished themselves from geoengineering, emphasizing that BECCS and other terrestrial negative emissions technologies should be considered as a form of mitigation. The merger was thus accompanied by an increasingly strong emphasis on divorcing CDR from SRM and a gradual abandonment of the overarching geoengineering term, evidence of which can be found in interviewees reflections about seemingly endless debates on how geoengineering technologies should best be named and categorized. This dynamic was further reinforced by the activities of critical communities like the advocacy organizations that continue highlighting the dangers of geoengineering. Their continued vocal engagement motivated researchers to highlight governance considerations and/or find different terms in order to avoid the controversy around geoengineering entirely. In this way, the geoengineering object became increasingly malleable and adaptable to different contexts.

The result becomes clearly visible when comparing the discussion on geoengineering in the IPCC's fifth assessment report (IPCC, 2013a) and its report on 1.5°C (IPCC, 2018). The former's summary for policymakers includes a paragraph on geoengineering, defining it as 'methods that aim to deliberately alter the climate system to counter climate change', but stating that '[l]limited evidence precludes a comprehensive quantitative assessment of both SRM and CDR and their impact on the climate system' (p. 29). The latter's summary for policymakers takes a different approach, distinguishing between mitigation, CDR, adaptation, and 'remedial measures' (equated with SRM), explicitly excluding the term 'geoengineering' (p. 70). In the report, we now see two entirely new climate change policy options that are no longer mentioned somewhere in a last paragraph, but side by side with the traditional categories of mitigation and adaptation.

3.4 Learning from the Case of Geoengineering

The analysis in this section describes how the internal dynamics of the geoengineering core community and its interaction with other communities led to transforming geoengineering into a distinct, salient, and malleable governance object. It shows that there was/is indeed a community of individuals that co-evolved with the geoengineering concept and that contributed to establishing it as an object of governance. It also highlights the important role of individuals who bridge different groups of scholars, and who introduce new colleagues to the subject using salient narratives of problems and solutions. Finally, it describes the important role of diversity and contestation for adapting the concept to different contexts and for making it 'travel'. This manifests in a constant changing of terminology and demarcation, often with an effort to adjust the object to the environment that it is being introduced to in order to avoid anticipated critique.

A key observation is that the distinctiveness, saliency, and eventual malleability of geoengineering was *co-produced* between those who advocated for the idea and those who opposed it. In the beginning, critics of geoengineering led members of the core community to create narratives of common cause, increasing internal cohesion and contributing to the use of a common language. At the same time, these critics themselves depended on a stable object to engage with, adding to the distinctiveness of the object with their own language and narratives. Critical narratives and the attention that both scholars and advocacy groups draw towards any activities that they label as 'geoengineering' also increases the saliency of the object towards actors outside the community, preventing it from becoming normalized and maintaining it as relevant and separate from other climate policies in policymaker circles. But their critical engagement has also evoked responses from geoengineering core community members. Because of this criticism, many geoengineering researchers have put governance questions at the front of their work, and in an effort to avoid further controversial attention, some avoid using the geoengineering term entirely. This in turn has contributed to the malleability of the object, enabling it to travel and adapt to different contexts.

What general lessons can we draw from this case? In this section, I have conceptualized the geoengineering core community as part of a larger knowledge network containing different groups that engage with geoengineering as a governance object. The knowledge network thus contains a wide variety of actors, some of whom could be considered part of an 'epistemic community' or 'invisible college', others who could be considered as a 'governance network' or a '(transnational) advocacy network'. What unites them is their effort to produce or shape knowledge about geoengineering, and their efforts to influence policy. In this sense, I consider a knowledge network to be similar or comparable to other issue networks that are active in global politics, and that the elementary processes of cohesion, brokerage, and diversity are generally relevant to all kinds of networks engaging in knowledge construction and policy influence.

With respect to cohesion, the geoengineering case then confirms findings about the importance of a shared language and problem definition. Maarten Hajer and Wytske Versteeg (2005) have argued that a shared discourse is essential to the success of what they call a 'governance network', describing how networks made up of very different actors gradually adopt not only a common policy language, but also a shared identification of core problems and potential solutions. According to them, 'it is the discourse that keeps the governance network together and explains the actions that the various participants see as appropriate' (p. 343). The geoengineering case adds further insight to how such a common discourse is upheld, namely by creating feelings of trust and togetherness amongst the members of a community, and, in some cases, by ostracizing those who question the community's cause. Yet, the geoengineering case also shows that cohesion and distinctiveness can be further enhanced by the activities of vocal critics who depend on a shared and stable governance object to engage with. The resulting cohesion enables the distinctiveness identified by Olaf Corry (2013) as important for generating successful governance objects.

With respect to brokerage, the similarity of framings in early seminal articles and the network's later discourses supports findings about the importance of so-called seed actors in shaping the content of the network's activity. In their study of the evolution of 'advocacy networks', David Lake and Wendy Wong (2009) argue that certain individuals serve as seeds around which a network clusters, and that these individuals shape the ends towards which the network collectively moves. The geoengineering case adds an important extension to this finding, namely that successful seed actors are required to continuously engage in expanding the knowledge network by introducing the idea to new audiences, and that they rely on attraction narratives to do this. In other words, a successful governance object needs to connect to and resonate with the ideas and structures present in different groups. A broker who understands the normative and institutional context of these groups can more easily adapt the definition or the narrative accompanying a governance object to fit different contexts. This reshaping of definitions and narratives according to context enables growth of the knowledge network and enhances the salience that is needed for a governance object to become relevant to political decision-making.

With respect to diversity, the importance of links to different organizations and societal realms supports findings about mechanisms of diffusion and success. In their analysis of transnational advocacy networks, Margaret Keck and Kathryn Sikkink (1999) reflect that these networks 'build new links among actors in civil society, states and international organizations', thereby multiplying opportunities for dialogue and exchange (p. 89). Witte et al., (2000) similarly posit that the distinctive flavour of what they call 'global public policy networks' is their ability to bring together actors from diverse backgrounds. Successful knowledge networks appear to be no different from these governance/policy/advocacy networks, in that they depend on members with connections to a broad set of organizations and societal realms for their ideas to spread and to turn into malleable, transportable objects of governance. At the same time, one kind of diversity does not equal another. Mai'A Davis Cross (2013) highlights social cohesion, personal relationships, and shared values as a key factor that determines the success and influence of a given community. As we have seen in the geoengineering knowledge network, its members are very homogeneous in some ways, including gender and geographical representation. This homogeneity facilitates the all important aspect of internal social cohesion, which brings us back to the first dynamic and explains how the community is able to collectively frame a certain social reality and thereby be more persuasive towards an external audience.

Going beyond the dynamics within one community, we can also learn from the dynamics that happen between different communities who engage in the same field. Rivalry of concepts and communities have played an important role in shaping the geoengineering governance object. Different communities, even if they are motivated by the same cause, identify themselves through the use of certain concepts. These concepts might refer to exactly the same thing (e.g., CDR vs. 'negative emissions technologies' vs. 'greenhouse gas removal'), but they indicate to the reader or listener which community the individual feels that he or she belongs to. Concepts like these provide a banner for communities to rally around, and the cohesion mechanisms that ensure the existence of the community make it difficult to rename those banners. Sometimes a community gets 'stuck' with an highly contested concept like geoengineering, and only the engagement with a rivalling community can lead to the creation of a new and more malleable framing of the governance object that finds sufficient acceptance. This points to a research agenda that goes beyond examining individual communities and concepts, towards understanding the dynamics of their interaction.

4 Historical and Cultural Contexts: A Critical Reflection

When we try to understand the emergence of a concept like geoengineering, accounting for process and the actions of networks and individuals is but one side of the story. There is an increasing consensus amongst scholars who study geoengineering from a critical perspective that the wider historical and cultural context matters greatly for explaining the emergence of this idea.

In a very cursory manner, I will therefore introduce three aspects of the larger history and context that have contributed to setting the stage for geoengineering to emerge. These include the conception of the climate as a global and digitally alterable object that evolved from using models in climatology; the colonial mindset that underpins suggestions to use large amounts of 'unused land' for carbon removal and that promotes stratospheric aerosol injection as a way to protect vulnerable communities; and the Anthropocentric narratives shared in Western contexts that stylize geoengineering as a way to save the environment, but that also highlight a stark difference in attitudes between Europe and the United States. This contextualization is by no means complete or exhaustive. It is expressly based on personal reflection, and it is only meant as a rough sketch of the wider background that (I believe) facilitated geoengineering to become a reasonable idea.

4.1 The World on a Computer Screen

Climatology as we know it today developed hand in hand with the invention of computers and profited enormously from military interest in the ability to predict weather. Paul Edwards (2010) provides a comprehensive analysis that should be read by all who are interested in this particular aspect of history. He explains how in the nineteenth century, climate science had relied primarily on qualitative approaches and regional studies of geography and natural history. Only around 1900 did climatologists start conceptualizing the climate as a global phenomenon that needed to be studied using global data, leaving the regional and geographical perspective they had taken earlier behind. The principal limitation at this time was the mathematical complexity of linking values and dependencies across time and space. This limitation changed gradually with the invention of computers during the World War II. Their potential to calculate complex patterns like weather made them highly interesting for military purposes, and between 1945 and 1965, their development was heavily supported by American military research agencies and the United States Weather Bureau. Useful weather prediction in turn was only possible using computer models that divide the planet into equally sized sections, using statistical extrapolations from recorded temperature and air pressure to predict weather in regions and times where little or no data is available. These models eventually provided the tools and principal ontological lens through which also climate science is approached today.

The twentieth-century shift from geographical to statistical methods and the use of computer models for climate science made it possible to extrapolate climates of the future from observations of the past and present. The models that enable this extrapolation have become increasingly complex, integrating global data from landscapes, oceans, solar activity, and industrial sectors. These Earth system models are nowadays at the core of climate science and constitute a key source of information for international climate negotiations and political decision-making. Not only do they provide estimates of future climates based on current values; they are also used in combination with economic models to calculate cost-benefit analyses of climate impacts and economic activity. Such cost-benefit analyses are in turn strongly dependent on the modelling team's world view about what factors to include and how to estimate their cost. Importantly, the economic models that they are combined with often follow a free market logic in that their principal aim is to minimize aggregate economic costs of mitigation and in that they typically assume fully functioning markets. This means that climate policy in such 'IAMs' is mainly interpreted as the implementation of a carbon price, largely ignoring other mechanisms by which social change may come about.

The centrality of IAMs in global climate knowledge and policymaking puts modellers into an unprecedented position of power, as the assumptions flowing into the model essentially define what is considered politically feasible. As Beck and Mahony (2017) explain, the work of the IPCC and particularly its central display of IAMs is highly performative, placing policy options that conform to the assumptions of the model on the table, and obscuring those that do not conform to the model's parameters. Key characteristics of contemporary climate science are thus its aggregate perspective on global systems, its (subjective) economic valuation of natural and social processes, and its scientific authority and power. Combined with the peculiar perspective that the use of computer models enables, namely to simulate any given climate at will by changing certain parameters in a digital representation of the Earth, this – in my opinion – has contributed to a perfect environment in which geoengineering could emerge.

Taking this environment into account, it is almost surprising that geoengineering solutions did not become more widespread earlier. Perhaps a principal reason for this is how the aim of the models developed over time (also see McLaren and Markusson, 2020). In earlier versions of IPCC reports (before 2007), IAMs had been used to calculate a set of different emissions scenarios that described general storylines of how society might develop in the future. They included variations in economic systems, population growth, local vs. global solutions to sustainability, and speeds of technological development. Their primary emphasis was thus the social dimension of climate change (IPCC, 2000). This changed in 2007, when the SRES models were replaced by so-called RCPs.[12] Rather than focusing on societal behaviour, the RCPs focused on

---

[12] The RCPs were one of two types of integrated assessment models developed to supersede the SRES models. The second type, the 'Shared Socioeconomic Pathways', were more similar to the SRES models in that they developed a set of socio-economic narratives. These were a lot more

the physical variable of radiative forcing. Instead of starting from present conditions and plotting forward into the future, they started with a future target and plotted backwards to find optimal policy pathways (Oreskes, 2015). In order to do this, the model needed to be fed with policy options that, in turn, were foreseen with an estimation of price and political feasibility. How these estimations are made has been subject to substantive critique (e.g., Workman et al., 2020), but the economically most affordable solutions that IAMs have produced for meeting low-temperature targets are the widespread use of bio-energy with CCS, large-scale afforestation, and – although always presented with reservations – stratospheric aerosol injection.

There is no question that climate science is necessary for informing climate policy, and that IAMs are invaluable for estimating what might be needed to prevent dangerous climate change. It is also natural that scientists, including climate modellers, have values and beliefs. What is problematic, however, is when highly authoritative scientific products that inherently depend on normative valuation of policy options are presented as value-free. This constitutes a dilemma for climate science and particularly for the IPCC (Havstad and Brown, 2017; Livingston et al., 2018). On the one hand, the IPCC faces a public expectation that its information is objective and neutral. At the same time, it is subject to pressure and scrutiny from governments worldwide to provide narratives of hope that will stimulate climate action and keep international negotiations going. This was particularly true in the build up and wake of the Paris Agreement, in which low-temperature pathways were in high demand. Yet in a normative context where ideas of sustainable development and economic growth provide the leitmotif of society, modellers end up playing the magician who is expected to pull a rabbit from a hat every time a new assessment report comes around. If economic growth and the Western style of living cannot be questioned or compromised, then the only solution to climate change is, indeed, geoengineering.

4.2 Colonial Legacies

It is difficult to understate the amount of land and resources needed to realize various proposals for geoengineering.[13] The RCPs of the Special Report on

---

complex and took more time to set up, which is why they are only used in IPCC assessments from 2020–21 onwards (Hausfather and Peters, 2020).

[13] While stratospheric aerosol injection would take place in the upper atmosphere and is not directly dependent on using land, some precipitation models indicate that certain regions in the world could be disproportionately affected by reductions in rainfall. Where these regions are depends on the location and concentration of the aerosols. For example, Sun *et al.* (2020) project that injection over the tropics could decrease precipitation in regions along the equator. Injection over the Arctic could suppress precipitation mainly in north-western Africa, central Asia, and

1.5°C require up to 6 million km^2 of additional land for bioenergy crops and up to 9.5 million km^2 for forests, relative to 2010. This projected necessity of large-scale carbon removal has resulted in a groundswell of 'net zero' targets by corporate actors. While vaguely defined, they share a core understanding that anthropogenic emissions of greenhouse gases will somehow be balanced by anthropogenic removals. Aims to compensate for greenhouse gas emissions through balancing, or 'offsetting', are taking on stupendous proportions. Greenpeace has reported that the 50Mha of land claimed for offsetting by a single company like Shell corresponds to about one tenth of globally available land that could be used without necessarily impacting food or biodiversity (Muttitt et al., 2021). Where these removals will take place is rarely made explicit. Yet because the land populated by societies with high levels of greenhouse gas emissions is often already saturated by intensive farming, the land-based removals needed to reach all these net zero goals are likely to require area that is not already categorized as intensely 'used' for other purposes.

The IPCC has estimated that a large proportion of land needed for carbon removals would come from reductions in pastures, of which up to 11 million km^2 (approximately one-fifth of global grassland area) would need to be converted to biomass production (IPCC, 2018, p. 16). A map of the distribution of cropland and grassland shows us that land used for pasture is situated primarily in the western part of North America, sub-Saharan Africa, South America, central Asia, and Australia (Figure 4). Notably, all of these regions have a history of foreign colonization and/or very low emissions per capita. In the United States, the area in question hosts almost all Native American communities. In Australia, the area in question hosts a large amount of exclusive or non-exclusive Aboriginal territory. In China, pastoral areas are mostly inhabited by Tibetan and Mongolian minorities. Meanwhile, the European Union is trying to stop any further decline of its grassland and pasture areas to protect biodiversity.

If not scrutinized carefully, this could essentially mean that once again, communities that have a history of being colonized and forced to move will likely end up providing the resources required to keep climate change at bay. That this connection is not more widely discussed demonstrates the depth and institutionalization of the colonial mindset. It is striking that our scientific and political leaders are comfortable with prioritizing solutions that would obviously require substantial behavioural and ecological change in the Global South, while discarding solutions that would require change to economic,

---

central America. However, the physics of how stratospheric aerosols could affect weather patterns is highly complex, and different studies produce widely differing estimates.

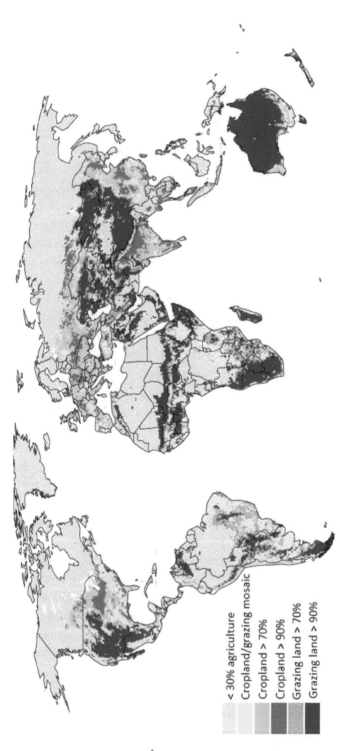

Figure 4 The majority of croplands (green) are spread out in the Northern Hemisphere, in the temperate zone, and in South and Eastern Asia. Areas covered by grasslands and pastures (brown) are dominant in Africa, South America, central Asia, and Australia.

Source: GRIDA (2006)

Legend:
- < 30% agriculture
- Cropland/grazing mosaic
- Cropland > 70%
- Cropland > 90%
- Grazing land > 70%
- Grazing land > 90%

agricultural, or individual behaviour in the Global North. The large majority of IPCC scenarios that stay below 1.5°C involve enormous amounts of BECCS and afforestation, but tend not to include much behavioural change. Upon critique, alternative models on the effects of behavioural change in consumption, travel and energy use by citizens in the Global North have been calculated (only possible after overriding the cost-optimization assumptions embedded in IAMs), showing that a minimization of BECCS and afforestation is indeed possible but would require substantial lifestyle changes in industrialized countries (Van Vuuren et al., 2018; Akenji et al., 2019).

Perhaps this is not very surprising considering the high concentration of Western perspectives in internationally relevant climate science. Yet instead of recognizing and addressing the colonial legacy embedded in climate change, much of the geoengineering governance literature has concerned itself with enabling public engagement and consultation on how to govern geoengineering research and deployment. This concern usually relates to geoengineering in a very isolated manner – Who should do the research? How should participation take place? How will deployment be conducted 'responsibly'?

Comparatively few studies in this field situate geoengineering in context with other climate solutions or in an historical context of responsibility for climate impacts (see Buck, 2016; Carton et al., 2020; Stephens and Surprise, 2020). Instead, proponents of geoengineering research tend to emphasize how geoengineering technologies would benefit vulnerable and Indigenous communities, and how those nations who are most threatened by climate change would likely be the ones most interested in a solution like stratospheric aerosol injection (Horton and Keith, 2016).

Survey data on perceptions in the Global South indicates that populations in developing and emerging economies, notably China, India, and the Philippines, might indeed be more open to geoengineering solutions than people in industrialized countries (Sugiyama et al., 2020). But what other perspectives are there on geoengineering and vulnerable communities? Kyle Powys Whyte (2019), citizen of the Potawatomi Nation and Professor of Environment and Sustainability at the University of Michigan, argues that from an Indigenous peoples perspective, it would be a fallacy to say that geoengineering saves vulnerable Indigenous communities from the impacts of climate change. To him, climate change impacts themselves are a continuation and intensification of capitalism and industrialization, inflicting violence and harm on Indigenous peoples. He also argues that it is not the impacts of climate change that are the main problem – rather, it is the restriction in capacity to adapt to them. If Indigenous peoples had not been displaced from their land, forced to live in ecologically endangered areas and been curtailed in their ability to migrate freely, they would never have become as vulnerable to the effects of climate change in the first place.

The extractive industries that cause climate change, as well as any solutions to climate change that infringe on the collective self-determination rights of Indigenous peoples, are processes that rely on colonial domination. Colonial legacies are thus fundamental to the full cycle of anthropogenic engagement with climate change: from the extraction of oil, gas, and coal (often in areas where Indigenous communities live), over the use of hydropower and externally determined forest conservation (often making Indigenous communities relocate), to the advocacy for bioenergy with CCS or stratospheric aerosol injection (requiring land and potentially affecting the distribution of rainfall in regions inhabited by Indigenous and non-Western populations). It seems like the entire cycle relies on perceiving the world as unclaimed territory that is available to serve the interests of an industrialized elite. This legacy is deeply embedded in Western thinking and seems to also constitute a foundation of contemporary climate science and policymaking.

4.3 Anthropocene Narratives

Geoengineering science and climate science are dominated by Western universities and Western perspectives. In the geoengineering knowledge network discussed in Section 3, about 75 per cent of researchers are based in OECD countries, two-thirds of whom work in the United States, the United Kingdom, and Germany (Biermann and Möller, 2019). Analyses of the IPCC show that the same proportions apply to climate science more broadly, highlighting the influence of North American and British institutions in training authors who write the chapter on mitigation options (Ho-Lem et al., 2011; Corbera et al., 2016). One can therefore presume that the scientific perspective on climate change is also characterized by a Western understanding of socio-ecological systems: that 'nature' is separate from humans, that it is both a physical object and a morally weighted property, and that humans are capable of and responsible for controlling, modifying and/or protecting it (Nielsen, 2014; McLaren and Corry, 2021b).

Yet within the Western perspective, there are important differences. A traditional fault line concerns the role and responsibility that humans have with respect to nature. In the bio-centric version of environmentalism, humans have a duty and obligation to reduce their impact on nature as much as possible, protecting nature from human intervention and enabling it to be untouched and wild. This perspective greatly informed Western environmental policy of the twentieth century, where national parks and reserves were a principal tool of realizing environmental protection around the world. With the rising debate on social justice and human rights in environmental management, particularly in relation to cases of land dispossession in the Global South, bio-centrism became increasingly criticized and left a space for more Anthropocentric understandings of nature protection (Dowie, 2010). In more recent versions of environmentalism, humans have the right, and the obligation, to use, shape, and improve the environment for both human and nature's sake. Instead of protecting nature by separating it from humans, nature is protected by actively tending to it.

It is no coincidence that the emergence of geoengineering happened in a period in which the 'Anthropocene' became a popular buzzword across science and policy, culminating in a proposal by a working group of the International Union of Geological Science to define it as an official epoch of the geologic time scale (Zalasiewicz et al., 2019). Paul Crutzen, the atmospheric chemist who coined the term 'Anthropocene' in 2002 and who is one of the thirty-four members of this working group, also played a central role in catalyzing the geoengineering discussion. The basic narrative of the Anthropocene is that humans have had such fundamental impacts on the Earth that there is no square metre of untouched nature left. At the same time, human populations and human impact are likely to continue rising, which is why the only way to save life on Earth is through the deliberate use of science and technology. This narrative constitutes the foundation of the 'Good Anthropocene', an era in which humankind becomes aware of the impacts that its use of science and technology has had, and learns to use them in a way that makes human life on Earth sustainable. Jeremy Baskin (2019) further unpacks this relationship in his book *Geoengineering, the Anthropocene and the End of Nature*.

While the idea of the 'good Anthropocene' has become increasingly popular in both Europe and the United States, differences in historical and normative context on the two sides of the Atlantic colour its interpretation. In Europe, the term 'geoengineering' and particularly the idea of stratospheric aerosol injection are often seen in a negative light. The idea of deliberate climate intervention at the global scale runs counter to deeply seated norms of prevention and precaution stemming from the more bio-centric perspective on nature – a legacy of Nordic and German public welfare policy from the 1970s that has become fundamental to both European and international environmental legislation (Sand, 2010). From interactions with European policymakers and scientists, my general impression is that geoengineering technologies are only considered a viable option if they resemble already established systems of tending to nature (such as forestry and nature restoration), or if they can be separated from natural systems and contained in the form of an industrial/ agricultural process (such as direct air CCS, or bioenergy with CCS). Where this takes place is of no great matter. European nations have a history of international trade and investment in agricultural and energy products, so assuming that nature-based or agro-industrial climate solutions will occur in different parts of the world is not particularly controversial.

The United States differs from the European context in that technological interventions into natural systems are much more widely accepted and institutionalized. In contrast to Europe, the United States follows a more liberal position in using technology to intervene in and improve the natural environment. This difference has been a fundamental bone of contention in international trade disputes and the regulation around genetically modified species (Van Den Belt and Gremmen, 2002), and it provides a similar context for geoengineering. Because the United States has a more daring approach to technological intervention, an idea like stratospheric aerosol injection can more easily be framed and accepted as necessary or desirable. Provided that the science behind it is sound, there is no immediate reason to discard it. In addition, the United States has a unique history of inciting and participating in international competition when it comes to races in grand technology, including the World War II race to nuclear power, the Cold War race to landing a man on the moon, and recently the race to artificial intelligence. Stratospheric aerosol injection, with its appeal to global power, falls neatly into this row of races and has already been framed as a matter of 'preventing rogue actors' and 'maintaining leadership' in US scientific assessments and hearings of Congress (Schubert, 2021).

In terms of understanding the emergence of governance objects, we must therefore also take into account the cultural foundations that enable or restrict different narratives. Where geoengineering has no doubt become a distinct and salient global governance object, the potential to also make it malleable may be restricted by differences in cultural foundations across countries. For a governance object to become successful by embodying all three characteristics, it must thus cater to a common cultural denominator of at least the most powerful nations in global climate politics. Given that these nations share widely shared ideals of capitalism and free markets, CDR with its link to carbon trading seems to have found such a common cultural denominator.

5 Conclusion

As the idea to engineer the climate is increasingly becoming part and parcel of contemporary climate policy, it is important to take a step back and reflect on where we are coming from and where we might be going. In this Element, I have asked questions about why scientists and policymakers began engaging with the geoengineering concept in the first place, what their role was in turning geoengineering into a governance object, and how redesigning the atmosphere came to be perceived as a reasonable or even unavoidable policy option.

In trying to find answers to these questions, I have argued that understanding the emergence of geoengineering as a governance object goes hand in hand with understanding the knowledge network that gathered around it. My analysis indicates that the (recent) evolution of geoengineering as a governance object is a product of the interaction between three distinct communities: a community of geoengineering researchers, a community of critical advocacy organizations, and a community of integrated assessment modellers. Using powerful attraction narratives, knowledge brokers in both the geoengineering community and the critical advocacy community introduced new audiences to a shared language and a set of common assumptions, compounding the distinctiveness and saliency of geoengineering. Confrontation with both internal and external criticism encouraged geoengineering researchers to make governance considerations central to their agenda. But the continued contestation of 'geoengineering' also motivated a catalogue of changing terminology and categorization to evade public critique. This development was reinforced by the interaction with a third community of integrated assessment modellers, who contributed to removing CDR from the umbrella term of geoengineering and making this form of Earth system engineering a separate and more malleable object of governance.

We can thus observe two contrasting but mutually reinforcing social dynamics that shape the emergence and evolution of geoengineering: one in which actors uphold geoengineering as a distinct and salient governance object that requires specialized attention and regulation, and one in which actors diffuse geoengineering into sub-techniques that become associated with different umbrella terms and therefore become a more 'normalized' part of climate policy and research. The struggle between these two dynamics is ongoing. With the integration of large-scale negative emissions technologies into the IPCC's emissions scenarios, the CDR part of what was once considered geoengineering is becoming part and parcel of the international climate policy portfolio. Also the SRM part is becoming somewhat more diffused and associated with umbrella terms like 'basic research', at least in the United States where there is some political and cultural support for this approach. With this diffusion of geoengineering, activists and advocacy organisations who question the basic premises of deliberate climate control are struggling to maintain a target for criticism, and their continued use of the geoengineering terminology is increasingly perceived to be radical and out of place. Yet they rely on maintaining this term in order to separate what they think is problematic about an Earth system engineering approach from other approaches to climate policy. The contestation of norms, or the struggle for what should be considered key principles of global environmentalism, thus remains at the heart of the geoengineering debate.

What does this case tell us about the emergence of global governance objects? In the introduction, I hypothesize that the characteristics of a successful global governance object – distinctiveness, salience, and malleability – might be the result of certain social network dynamics that take place within a 'successful' knowledge network, and that such knowledge networks are ultimately the source of such governance objects. My analysis indicates that a knowledge network was indeed involved in shaping geoengineering as a governance object, and that dynamics like cohesion, brokerage, and diversity did have an important role to play. But it also highlights the key importance of *interaction* between different communities within the network, showing how contestation and critique contributed to making geoengineering distinctive and salient. In the end however, this controversial governance object needed to develop into something more culturally palatable across nations in order to actually become an integrated part of policymaking. We can thus conclude that in order to understand why we govern the things we do, it is not enough to look at individual governance objects or communities. The key to understanding change and evolution in global governance is to look at their context and their interaction.

It is worth noting that the story of how geoengineering became a global governance object is not unique. Similar processes can be found in many other cases where new resource frontiers are being explored, and in any place where access is possible primarily through scientific methods and tools. From deep-sea fishing to extraterrestrial mining and from nuclear fission to artificial intelligence, knowledge networks that form around any given frontier have argued that its imminent exploitation calls for more scientific research and an urgent need to form governance mechanisms. The research of a new frontier thus goes hand in hand with the creation of a governance object, paving the way for wider societal engagement and, in many cases, enabling the successful exploitation of the resource. Geoengineering is only one example in this row of frontiers, turning the atmosphere itself into a resource that can be used to fulfil the needs an ever-growing economy. Science has traditionally been the pioneering force that opens up new frontiers for colonization and industrial use, and it continues to do so today.

If we accept this phenomenon as a repeating pattern, then there is little use in criticizing the process itself. What we can be critical about is *what* scientific research chooses to measure and *how* it defines the object that is to be governed. Currently, geoengineering technologies are being imagined and designed with the primary intention of reducing global average temperatures in the face of what appear to be prohibitively high costs for rapid emissions reductions. They arise out of an ontological setting in which the atmosphere can be altered at will behind a computer screen, and in which the unpredictable nature of politics and people plays a marginal role. This way of conceptualizing the frontier hides very real risks, especially if it lends the impression that techno-scientific solutions are easier or more feasible than policies which require behavioural change. In the end, any solution – particularly at this scale – will require substantial changes in behaviour. And it may well be that, although BECCS, afforestation and stratospheric aerosol injection look like feasible and affordable measures today, the comparatively marginal role that is attributed to their societal dimensions will come to bite us from behind in the future. Meanwhile, precious time may be lost by choosing to believe that the magician's rabbit is real and not just a pleasant illusion.

Despite finally having an international agreement that includes ambitious temperature targets, we need to remember that climate change is not only about temperatures or concentrations of carbon dioxide. Geographers like Mike Hulme (2014) remind us that a changing climate is about changes in the local environment and how these changes affect the values and structures of societies. As this Element shows, values and societal structures also lie at the heart of the geoengineering debate. Recognizing and openly embracing this observation is and will continue to be key for situating and understanding the past, current, and future role of geoengineering within the wider setting of Earth System Governance.

References

Akenji, L, Lettenmeier, M., Toivio, V., Koide, R., and Amellina, A. (2019) *1.5-Degree Lifestyles: Targets and Options for Reducing Lifestyle Carbon Footprints. Technical Report*. Hayama, Japan.

Allan, B. B. (2017) 'Producing the Climate: States, Scientists, and the Constitution of Global Governance Objects', *International Organization*, 71(1), pp. 131–62.

Anderson, K. and Peters, G. (2016) 'The Trouble with Negative Emissions', *Science*, 354(6309), pp. 182–3. https://doi.org/10.1126/science.aah4567.

Anshelm, J. and Hansson, A. (2014a) 'Battling Promethean Dreams and Trojan Horses: Revealing the Critical Discourses of Geoengineering', *Energy Research & Social Science*, 2(2014), pp. 135–44.

Anshelm, J. and Hansson, A. (2014b) 'The Last Chance to Save the Planet? An Analysis of the Geoengineering Advocacy Discourse in the Public Debate', *Environmental Humanities*, 5(2014), pp. 101–23.

Antoniades, A. (2003) 'Epistemic Communities, Epistemes and the Construction of (World) Politics', *Global Society*, 17(1), pp. 21–38. https://doi.org/10.1080/0953732032000053980.

Arrhenius, S. (1908) *Worlds in the Making: The Evolution of the Universe*. New York: Harper & Brothers.

Asayama, S. et al. (2019) 'Beyond Solutionist Science for the Anthropocene: To Navigate the Contentious Atmosphere of Solar Geoengineering', *The Anthropocene Review*, 6(2), pp. 19–37. https://doi.org/10.1177/2053019619843678.

Baskin, J. (2019) *Geoengineering, the Anthropocene and the End of Nature, Geoengineering, the Anthropocene and the End of Nature*. Cham, Switzerland: Palgrave Macmillan. https://doi.org/10.1007/978-3-030-17359-3_1.

Beck, S. et al. (2014) 'Towards a Reflexive Turn in the Governance of Global Environmental Expertise the Cases of the IPCC and the IPBES', *GAIA – Ecological Perspectives for Science and Society*, 23(2), pp. 80–7. https://doi.org/10.14512/gaia.23.2.4.

Beck, S. and Mahony, M. (2017) 'The IPCC and the Politics of Anticipation', *Nature Publishing Group*, 7(5), pp. 311–3. https://doi.org/10.1038/nclimate3264.

Belter, C. W. and Seidel, D. J. (2013) 'A Bibliometric Analysis of Climate Engineering Research', *Wiley Interdisciplinary Reviews: Climate Change*, 4(5), pp. 417–27. https://doi.org/10.1002/wcc.229.

Benjamin, L. and Thomas, A. (2016) '1.5 To Stay Alive? AOSIS and the Long Term Temperature Goal in the Paris Agreement', *SSRN Working Paper*, 3392503, 122–9.

Bennett, A. and George, A. (1997) *Process Tracing in Case Study Research*. Washington, DC: McArthur Program on Case Studies.

Biermann, F. and Möller, I. (2019) 'Rich Man's Solution? Climate Engineering Discourses and the Marginalization of the Global South', *International Environmental Agreements: Politics, Law and Economics*, 19(2), pp. 151–67. https://doi.org/10.1007/s10784-019-09431-0.

Biermann, F. et al. (2022) 'Solar Geoengineering: The Case for an International Non-Use Agreement', *Wiley Interdisciplinary Reviews: Climate Change*, e754, pp. 1–8. https://doi.org/10.1002/WCC.754.

Black, R. et al. (2021) *Taking Stock: A Global Assessment of Net Zero Targets*. https://ec.europa.eu/clima/policies/strategies/2050_en (Accessed 28 April 2021).

Boettcher, M. (2020) 'Cracking the Code: How Discursive Structures Shape Climate Engineering Research Governance', *Environmental Politics*, 29(5), pp. 890–916. https://doi.org/10.1080/09644016.2019.1670987.

Borgatti, S. P., Mehra, A., Brass, D. J., and Labianca, G. (2009) 'Network Analysis in the Social Sciences', *Science*, *323*(5916), pp. 892–5. https://doi .org/10.1126/science.1165821

Boyd, E., Corbera, E. and Estrada, M. (2008) 'UNFCCC Negotiations (pre-Kyoto to COP-9): What the Process Says about the Politics of CDM-sinks', *International Environmental Agreements: Politics, Law and Economics*, 8(2), pp. 95–112. https://doi.org/10.1007/s10784-008-9070-x.

Buck, H. J. (2016) 'Rapid Scale-up of Negative Emissions Technologies: Social Barriers and Social Implications', *Climatic Change*, 139, pp. 155–67. https:// doi.org/10.1007/s10584-016-1770-6.

Buck, H. J. (2019) *After Geoengineering: Climate Tragedy, Repair and Restoration*. London: Verso.

Buck, H. J., Gammon, A. R. and Preston, J. (2014) 'Gender and Geoengineering', *Hypatia*, 29(3), pp. 621–69. https://doi.org/10.1111/hypa.12083.

Bundesregierung (2012) 'Antwort der Bundesregierung auf die Kleine Anfrage der Abgeordneten René Röspel, Dr. Ernst Dieter Rossmann, Oliver Kaczmarek, weiterer Abgeordneter und der Fraktion der SPD – Drucksache 17/9943 – Geoengineering/Climate-Engineering'.

Burns, W. C. G. and Nicholson, S. (2015) 'Introduction to the Special Issue: Climate Engineering Law', *Climate Law*, 5(2–4), pp. 105–10. https://doi.org/ 10.1163/18786561-00504001.

Burt, R. S. (2005) *Brokerage and Closure: An Introduction to Social Capital*. New York: Oxford University Press.

Carton, W. (2019) '"Fixing" Climate Change by Mortgaging the Future: Negative Emissions, Spatiotemporal Fixes, and the Political Economy of Delay', *Antipode*, 51(3), pp. 750–69. https://doi.org/10.1111/ANTI.12532.

Carton, W. (2021) 'Carbon Unicorns and Fossil Futures', in Sapinski, J. P., Buck, H. J., and Malm, A. (eds.), *Has it come to this? The Promises and Perils of Geoengineering on the Brink*. New Brunswick, Canada: Rutgers University Press, pp. 34–49.

Carton, W., Lund, J. F. and Dooley, K. (2021) 'Undoing Equivalence: Rethinking Carbon Accounting for Just Carbon Removal', *Frontiers in Climate*, 3(664130), pp. 1–7. https://doi.org/10.3389/FCLIM.2021 .664130.

Carton, W. et al. (2020) 'Negative Emissions and the Long History of Carbon Removal', *Wiley Interdisciplinary Reviews: Climate Change*, 11(e671), pp. 1–25. https://doi.org/10.1002/WCC.671.

Climate Change Committee (2019) *Net Zero – Technical Report*. www .theccc.org.uk/publication/net-zero-technical-report/ (Accessed 5 February 2021).

Cohen-Sacham, E. et al. (2016) *Nature-based Solutions to Address Global Societal Challenges*. Gland, Switzerland. https://serval.unil.ch/resource/ serval:BIB_93FD38C8836B.P001/REF (Accessed: 8 June 2021).

Cointe, B., Cassen, C. and Nadaï, A. (2019) 'Organising Policy-Relevant Knowledge for Climate Action: Integrated Assessment Modelling, the IPCC, and the Emergence of a Collective Expertise on Socioeconomic Emission Scenarios', *Science and Technology Studies*, 32(4), pp. 36–57. https://doi.org/10.23987/sts.65031.

Collier, D. (2011) 'Understanding Process Tracing', *PS: Political Science & Politics*, 44(4), pp. 823–30. https://doi.org/10.1017/S1049096511001429.

Corbera, E. et al. (2016) 'Patterns of Authorship in the IPCC Working Group III Report', *Nature Climate Change*, 6(1), pp. 94–99. https://doi.org/10.1038/ nclimate2782.

Corry, O. (2013) *Constructing a Global Polity: Theory, Discourse and Governance*. Basingstoke, UK: Palgrave Macmillan. https://doi.org/10 .1057/9781137313652.

Cressey, D. (2012) *Geoengineering experiment cancelled amid patent row, Nature News*. www.nature.com/articles/nature.2012.10645.pdf (Accessed 23 August 2022).

Cross, M. K. D. (2013) 'Rethinking Epistemic Communities Twenty Years Later', *Review of International Studies*, 39(1), pp. 137–60. https://doi.org/10 .1017/S0260210512000034.

Crutzen, P. J. (2006) 'Albedo Enhancement by Stratospheric Sulfur Injections: A Contribution to Resolve a Policy Dilemma?', *Climatic Change*, 77(3–4), pp. 211–20. https://doi.org/10.1007/s10584-006-9101-y.

Darby, M. (2019) *Net Zero: The Story of the Target that will Shape our Future, Climate Home News.* www.climatechangenews.com/2019/09/16/net-zero-story-target-will-shape-future/ (Accessed 3 August 2022).

de Coninck, H. et al. (2018) 'Strengthening and Implementing the Global Response', in Masson-Delmotte, V. et al. (eds.), *Global Warming of 1.5°C. An IPCC Special Report on the impacts of global warming of 1.5°C above pre-industrial levels and related global greenhouse gas emission pathways.* Geneva: Intergovernmental Panel on Climate Change, pp. 313–443.

Dooley, K. and Gupta, A. (2017) 'Governing by Expertise: The Contested Politics of (Accounting for) Land-Based Mitigation in a New Climate Agreement', *International Environmental Agreements: Politics, Law and Economics*, 17(4), pp. 483–500. https://doi.org/10.1007/S10784-016-9331-Z/TABLES/1.

Dowie, M. (2010) *Conservation Refugees: The Hundred-Year Conflict between Global Conservation and Native Peoples.* Cambridge, MA: MIT Press.

Doyle, A. (2020) *Planned Harvard balloon test in Sweden stirs solar geoengineering unease | Reuters, Reuters.* www.reuters.com/article/us-climate-change-geoengineering-trfn-idUSKBN28S232 (Accessed 10 June 2021).

Earth Negotiations Bulletin (2019) *Summary of the Fourth Session of the United Nations Environment Assembly: 11–15 March 2019.* https://enb.iisd.org/events/4th-meeting-oecpr-and-4th-session-unea/summary-report-11-15-march-2019 (Accessed: 8 June 2021).

Edenhofer, O. et al. (2012) *IPCC Expert Meeting on Geoengineering Meeting Report.* www.ipcc.ch/ (Accessed 1 June 2021).

Edwards, P. N. (2010). *A Vast Machine: Computer Models, Climate Data, and the Politics of Global Warming.* Cambridge, MA: MIT Press. https://mitpress.mit.edu/9780262518635/a-vast-machine/

ETC Group (2010) *Geopiracy: The Case Against Geoengineering.* www.cbd.int/doc/emerging-issues/etcgroup-geopiracy-2011-013-en.pdf www.etcgroup.org (Accessed 3 June 2021).

Exxon research and engineering company (1982) *CO2 Greenhouse Gas Effect: A Technical Review, Climate Files.* www.climatefiles.com/exxonmobil/1982-memo-to-exxon-management-about-co2-greenhouse-effect/ (Accessed 23 August 2022).

Falkner, R. and Buzan, B. (2019) 'The Emergence of Environmental Stewardship as a Primary Institution of Global International Society', *European Journal of International Relations*, 25(1), pp. 131–55. https://doi.org/10.1177/1354066117741948.

Finnemore, M. and Sikkink, K. (1998) 'International Norm Dynamics and Political Change', *International Organization*, 52(4), pp. 887–917. https://doi.org/10.1162/002081898550789.

Flynn, J., Slovic, P. and Mertz, C. K. (1994) 'Gender, Race, and Perception of Environmental Health Risks', *Risk Analysis*, 14(6), pp. 1101–8. https://doi.org/10.1111/J.1539-6924.1994.TB00082.X.

Fountain, H. and Flavelle, C. (2021) 'Test Flight for Sunlight-Blocking Research Is Canceled – The New York Times', *New York Times*, 2 April. www.nytimes.com/2021/04/02/climate/solar-geoengineering-block-sunlight.html (Accessed 10 June 2021).

Freeman, L. C. (1979) 'Centrality in Social Networks Conceptual Clarification', *Social Networks*, 1(3), pp. 215–39. https://doi.org/10.1016/0378-8733(78)90021-7.

Friedkin, N. (2004) 'Social Cohesion', *Annual Review of Sociology*, 30(2004), pp. 409–25. https://doi.org/10.1146/annurev.soc.30.012703.110625.

Fuentes-George, K. (2017) 'Consensus, Certainty, and Catastrophe: Discourse, Governance, and Ocean Iron Fertilization', *Global Environmental Politics*, 17(2), pp. 125–43. https://doi.org/10.1162/GLEP.

Fuss, S. et al. (2020) 'Moving toward Net-Zero Emissions Requires New Alliances for Carbon Dioxide Removal', *One Earth*, 3(2), pp. 145–9. https://doi.org/10.1016/J.ONEEAR.2020.08.002.

Galaz, V. (2021, March 9) 'Naivt att tillåta klimatmanipulation'. *Svenska Dagbladet*. www.svd.se/a/zg6ko5/naivt-att-tillata-klimatmanipulation (Accessed 14 November.2022).

Gannon, K. E. and Hulme, M. (2018) 'Geoengineering at the "Edge of the World": Exploring Perceptions of Ocean Fertilisation through the Haida Salmon Restoration Corporation', *Geo: Geography and Environment*, 5(1), pp. 1–21. https://doi.org/10.1002/GEO2.54.

Geoengineering Monitor (2021) *SCoPEx in Sweden: First Step Down the Slippery Slope of Risky Solar Geoengineering Experiments – Geoengineering Monitor*. www.geoengineeringmonitor.org/2020/12/scopex-in-sweden-first-step-down-the-slippery-slope-of-risky-solar-geoengineering-experiments/ (Accessed 10 June 2021).

George, A. L. and Bennett, A. (2005) *Case Studies and Theory Development in the Social Sciences*. Cambridge, MA: The Belfer Center for Science and International Affairs.

Ginzky, H. and Frost, R. (2014) 'Marine Geo-Engineering: Legally Binding Regulation under the London Protocol', *Carbon & Climate Law Review*, 8(2), pp. 82–96.

Goodell, J. (2010) *A Hard Look at the Perils and Potential of Geoengineering, Yale Environment.* https://e360.yale.edu/features/a_hard_look_at_the_perils_ and_potential_of_geoengineering (Accessed 23 August 2022).

Govindasamy, B. and Caldeira, K. (2000) 'Geoengineering Earth's Radiation Balance to Mitigate CO2-induced Climate Change', *Geophysical Research Letters*, 27(14), pp. 2141–4. https://doi.org/10.1029/1999GL006086.

Granovetter, M. S. (1973) 'The Strength of Weak Ties', *Am J Sociol American Journal of Sociology*, 78(6), pp. 1360–80. https://doi.org/10.1086/225469.

Muttitt, G., Kronick, C., and Rouse, L. (2021) *Net Expectations: Assessing the Role of Carbon Dioxide Removal in Companies' Climate Plans.* London: Greenpeace.

GRIDA (2006) *Agriculture Land Use Distribution –Croplands and Pastures, Global Environmental Outlook 4 (GEO-4). Cartographer: This.* www .grida.no/resources/5531 (Accessed 14 November 2022).

Guest, G., Namey, E. E., and Mitchell, M. L. (2013) 'Participant Observation', in Guest, G., Namey, E. E., & Mitchell, M. L. (eds.), *Collecting Qualitative Data: A Field Manual for Applied Research* (pp. 75–112). London: SAGE. https://doi.org/10.4135/9781506374680.N3

Gupta, A. and Möller, I. (2019) 'De Facto Governance: How Authoritative Assessments Construct Climate Engineering as an Object of Governance', *Environmental Politics*, 28(3), pp. 480–501. https://doi.org/10.1080/09644 016.2018.1452373.

Gutiérrez, M. et al. (2014) *Summary of the Twelfth Session of Working Group III of the Intergovernmental Panel on Climate Change (IPCC) and the Thirty-Ninth Session of the IPCC: 7–12 April 2014.* www.iisd.ca/climate/ipcc39/ (Accessed 20 May 2021).

Haas, P. M. (1992a) 'Banning Chlorofluorocarbons: Epistemic Community Efforts to Protect Stratospheric Ozone', *International Organization*, 46(1), pp. 187–224. https://doi.org/10.1017/S002081830000148X.

Haas, P. M. (1992b) 'Introduction: Epistemic Communities and International Policy Coordination', *Knowledge, Power, and International Policy Coordination*, 46(1), pp. 1–35. https://doi.org/10.1017/S00208183000 01442.

Hajer, M. and Versteeg, W. (2005) 'Performing Governance through Networks', *European Political Science*, 4(3), pp. 340–7. https://doi.org/10.1057/ palgrave.eps.2210034.

Hausfather, Z. and Peters, G. P. (2020) 'Emissions – The "Business as Usual" Story is Misleading', *Nature*, 577(7792), pp. 618–20. https://doi.org/10.1038/ d41586-020-00177-3.

Havstad, J. C. and Brown, M. J. (2017) 'Neutrality, Relevance, Prescription, and the IPCC', *Public Affairs Quarterly*, 31(4), pp. 303–24. https://doi.org/10.2307/44732800.

Ho-Lem, C., Zerriffi, H. and Kandlikar, M. (2011) 'Who Participates in the Intergovernmental Panel on Climate Change and Why: A Quantitative Assessment of the National Representation of Authors in the Intergovernmental Panel on Climate Change', *Global Environmental Change*, 21(4), pp. 1308–17. https://doi.org/10.1016/j.gloenvcha.2011.05.007.

Horton, J. B. and Keith, D. (2016) 'Solar Geoengineering and Obligations to the Global Poor', in Preston, C. (ed.), *Climate Justice and Geoengineering: Ethics and Policy in the Atmospheric Anthropocenein the Atmospheric*. London: Rowman & Littlefield International, pp. 79–92.

House of Commons (2009) *Engineering: turning ideas into reality – Innovation, Universities, Science and Skills Committee*. https://publications.parliament.uk/pa/cm200809/cmselect/cmdius/50/50i.pdf (Accessed 1 June 2021).

House of Commons (2010) *The Regulation of Geoengineering*. Science and Technology Committee, Session 2009–10, 10. March. https://publications.parliament.uk/pa/cm200910/cmselect/cmsctech/221/221.pdf (Accessed 14 November 2022).

Hulme, M. (2014) *Can Science Fix Climate Change?* Cambridge: Polity Press.

Ingold, K. and Pflieger, G. (2016) 'Two Levels, Two Strategies: Explaining the Gap Between Swiss National and International Responses Toward Climate Change', *European Policy Analysis*, 2(1), pp. 20–38. https://doi.org/10.18278/EPA.2.1.4.

IPCC (1990) *Climate Change: The IPCC Scientific Assessment*. Edited by J. T. Houghton, G. J. Jenkins, and J. J. Ephraums. Cambridge: Cambridge University Press.

IPCC (2000) *Special Report on Emissions Scenarios*. Edited by N. Nakicenovic and R. Swart. Cambridge: Cambridge University Press.

IPCC (2013a) *Climate Change 2013: The Physical Science Basis. Contribution of Working Group I to the Fifth Assessment Report of the Intergovernmental Panel on Climate Change*. Edited by T. F. Stocker et al. Cambridge: Cambridge University Press.

IPCC (2013b) 'WG1 Summary for Policymakers', in Stocker, T. F., D. Qin, G.-K. Plattner, M. et al. (ed.), *Climate Change 2013: The Physical Science Basis. Contribution of Working Group 1 to the Fifth Assessment Report of the Intergovernmental Panel on Climate Change*. Cambridge: Cambridge University Press, pp 1–29.

IPCC (2014a) *Climate Change 2014: Mitigation of Climate Change. Contribution of Working Group III to the Fifth Assessment Report of the Intergovernmental Panel on Climate Change.* Edited by O. Edenhofer et al. Cambridge: Cambridge University Press.

IPCC (2014b) *Climate Change 2014: Synthesis Report. A Report of the Intergovernmental Panel on Climate Change.* Geneva: World Meteorological Organization.

IPCC (2018) 'Summary for Policymakers', in Masson-Delmotte, V., P. Zhai, H.-O. Pörtner, D. et al. (eds.), *Global Warming of 1.5°C. An IPCC Special Report on the impacts of global warming of 1.5°C above pre-industrial levels and related global greenhouse gas emission pathways, in the context of strengthening the global response to the threat of climate change.* Geneva: World Meteorological Organization, pp. 1–24.

Jamieson, D. (1996) 'Ethics and Intentional Climate Change', *Climatic Change*, 33(3), pp. 323–36. https://doi.org/10.1007/BF00142580.

Jones, N. (2018) 'Safeguarding Against Environmental Injustice: 1.5°C Scenarios, Negative Emissions, and Unintended Consequences', *Carbon & Climate Law Review*, 12(1), pp. 23–30. https://doi.org/10.21552/cclr/2018/1/6.

Keck, M. E. and Sikkink, K. (1999) 'Transnational Advocacy Networks in International and Regional Politics', *International Social Science Journal*, 51(159), pp. 89–101. https://doi.org/10.1111/1468-2451.00179.

Keith, D. W. (2000) 'Geoengineering the Climate: History and Prospect', *Annual Review of Energy and Environment*, 25, pp. 245–84. https://doi.org/10.1146/annurev.energy.25.1.245.

Keith, D. W. and Dowlatabadi, H. (1992) 'A Serious Look at Geoengineering', *Eos, Transactions, American Geophysical Union*, 73(27), pp. 289 and 292–3. https://doi.org/10.1029/91EO00231.

Kessler, J. (2019) *Novel Non-State Sources of De Facto Governance in the Solar Geoengineering Governance Landscape: The Case of SRMGI and C2G.* Wageningen, the Netherlands: Wageningen University and Research.

Keutsch, F. (2020) *Letter from Frank Keutsch to SCoPEx Advisory Committee, SCoPEx.* https://scopexac.com/wp-content/uploads/2020/12/Response-to-Sweden-Memo-9-Dec-2020.pdf (Accessed 10 June 2021).

Kintisch, E. (2010) *Hack the Planet.* Hoboken, New Jersey: John Wiley & Sons.

Köberle, A. C. (2019) 'The Value of BECCS in IAMs: a Review', *Current Sustainable/Renewable Energy Reports*, 6(4), pp. 107–15. https://doi.org/10.1007/s40518-019-00142-3.

Kraxner, F., Nilsson, S. and Obersteiner, M. (2003) 'Negative Emissions from BioEnergy Use, Carbon Capture and Sequestration (BECS) – The Case of

Biomass Production by Sustainable Forest Management from Semi-Natural Temperate Forests', *Biomass and Bioenergy*, 24, pp. 285–96. https://doi.org/10.1016/S0961-9534(02)00172-1.

Kreuter, J. (2021) *Climate Engineering as an Instance of Politicization: Talking Tomorrow's Technology – Framing Political Choice?* Cham, Switzerland: Springer.

Lake, D. A. and Wong, W. H. (2009) 'The Politics of Networks: Interests, Power, and Human Rights Norms', in Kahler, M. (ed.), *Networked Politics: Agency, Power, and Governance.* Ithaca, NY: Cornell University Press, pp. 127–50.

Lawrence, M. G. and Crutzen, P. J. (2017) 'Was Breaking the Taboo on Research on Climate Engineering Via Albedo Modification a Moral Hazard, or a Moral Imperative?' *Earth's Future*, 5, pp. 136–43. https://doi.org/10.1002/eft2.172.

Lenton, T. M. et al. (2008) 'Tipping Elements in the Earth's Climate System', *Proceedings of the National Academy of Sciences of the United States of America*, 105(6), pp. 1786–93. https://doi.org/10.1073/pnas.0705414105.

Livingston, J. E., Lövbrand, E. and Alkan Olsson, J. (2018) 'From Climates Multiple to Climate Singular: Maintaining Policy-Relevance in the IPCC Synthesis Report', *Environmental Science & Policy*, 90, pp. 83–90. https://doi.org/10.1016/J.ENVSCI.2018.10.003.

Livingston, J. E. and Rummukainen, M. (2020) 'Taking Science by Surprise: The Knowledge Politics of the IPCC Special Report on 1.5 Degrees', *Environmental Science and Policy*, 112, pp. 10–6. https://doi.org/10.1016/j.envsci.2020.05.020.

Lövbrand, E. (2011) 'Science and Public Policy Co-producing European Climate Science and Policy: A Cautionary Note on the Making of Useful Knowledge', *Science and Public Policy*, 38(3), pp. 225–36. https://doi.org/10.3152/030234211X12924093660516.

Lövbrand, E. et al. (2015) 'Who Speaks for the Future of Earth? How Critical Social Science can Extend the Conversation on the Anthropocene', *Global Environmental Change*, 32, pp. 211–8. https://doi.org/10.1016/j.gloenvcha.2015.03.012.

Low, S. and Schäfer, S. (2019) 'Tools of the Trade: Practices and Politics of Researching the Future in Climate Engineering', *Sustainability Science*, 14(4), pp. 953–62. https://doi.org/10.1007/s11625-019-00692-x.

MacCracken, M. C. (1991) 'Geoengineering the Climate', in *Workshop on the Engineering Response to Global Climate Change for Chapter 8: Control of Greenhouse Gas Sinks and of Climate.* Palm Coast, FL: Lawrence Livermore National Laboratory, pp. 1–13.

Marchetti, C. (1977) 'On Geoengineering and the CO2 Problem', *Climatic Change*, 1(1), pp. 59–68. https://doi.org/10.1007/BF00162777.

Markusson, N., McLaren, D. and Tyfield, D. (2018) 'Towards a Cultural Political Economy of Mitigation Deterrence by Negative Emissions Technologies (NETs)', *Global Sustainability*, 1(e10), pp. 1–9. https://doi.org/10.1017/SUS.2018.10.

Martin, J. H. (1990) 'Glacial-Interglacial CO2 Change: The Iron Hypothesis', *Paleoceanography*, 5(1), pp. 1–13. https://doi.org/10.1029/PA005i001p00001.

Matsuo, N. (2003) 'CDM in the Kyoto Negotiations: How CDM has Worked as a Bridge between Developed and Developing Worlds?' *Mitigation and Adaptation Strategies for Global Change*, 8(3), pp. 191–200. https://doi.org/10.1023/B:MITI.0000005638.74001.45.

Matthews, H. D. and Caldeira, K. (2008) 'Stabilizing Climate Requires Near-Zero Emissions', *Geophysical Research Letters*, 35(4), p. 4705. https://doi.org/10.1029/2007GL032388.

McKibben, B. (2021, March 3) 'Kulturdebatt. Det amerikanska experimentet med Kirunas himmel kan få katastrofala följder.' *Dagens Nyheter*. https://www.dn.se/kultur/det-amerikanska-experimentet-med-kirunas-himmel-kan-fa-katastrofala-foljder/ (Accessed 14 November 2022).

McKinnon, C. (2019) 'The Panglossian Politics of the Geoclique', *Critical Review of International Social and Political Philosphy*, 23(5), pp. 584–99. https://doi.org/10.1080/13698230.2020.1694216.

McLaren, D. and Corry, O. (2021a) 'Clash of Geofutures and the Remaking of Planetary Order: Faultlines underlying Conflicts over Geoengineering Governance', *Global Policy*, 12(S1), pp. 20–33. https://doi.org/10.1111/1758-5899.12863.

McLaren, D. and Corry, O. (2021b) 'The Politics and Governance of Research into Solar Geoengineering', *Wiley Interdisciplinary Reviews: Climate Change*, 12(3), p. e707. https://doi.org/10.1002/WCC.707.

McLaren, D. and Markusson, N. (2020) 'The Co-Evolution of Technological Promises, Modelling, Policies and Climate Change Targets', *Nature Climate Change*, 10(5), pp. 392–7. https://doi.org/10.1038/s41558-020-0740-1.

McLaren, D. et al. (2019) 'Beyond "Net-Zero": A Case for Separate Targets for Emissions Reduction and Negative Emissions', *Frontiers in Climate*, 1(4), pp. 1–5. https://doi.org/10.3389/fclim.2019.00004.

McNutt, M. K. et al. (2015) *Climate Intervention: Reflecting Sunlight to Cool Earth*. Washington, DC: The National Academies Press.

Möller, I. (2020) 'Political Perspectives on Geoengineering: Navigating Problem Definition and Institutional Fit', *Global Environmental Politics*, 20(2), pp. 57–82. https://doi.org/10.1162/glep_a_00547.

National Academy of Sciences (1992) *Policy Implications of Greenhouse Warming: Mitigation, Adaptation, and the Science Base*, Evans, D. J. (ed.). Washington, DC: National Academies Press. https://doi.org/10.17226/1605.

National Academy of Sciences (2015) *Report in Brief: Climate Intervention.* https://nap.nationalacademies.org/resource/18988/climate-intervention-brief-final.pdf (Accessed 23 August 2022).

Natural Environment Research Council (2009) *Geoengineering Scoping Workshop.* www.epsrc.ac.uk/newsevents/pubs/geoengineering-scoping-workshop-outputs/ (Accessed 9 February 2022).

New Climate Institute (2022) *Corporate Climate Responsibility Monitor 2022.* https://newclimate.org/2022/02/07/corporate-climate-responsibility-monitor-2022/ (Accessed 9 February 2022).

Nielsen, L. W. (2014) 'The "Nature" of "Nature": The Concept of Nature and Its Complexity in a Western Cultural and Ethical Context', *Global Bioethics*, 17(1), pp. 31–8. https://doi.org/10.1080/11287462.2004.10800840.

Nierenberg, W. A. et al. (1983) *Changing Climate: Report of the Carbon Dioxide Assessment Committee.* Washington, DC: The National Academies Press.

Obersteiner, M. et al. (2001, December) *Managing Climate Risk.* https://pure.iiasa.ac.at/id/eprint/6471/1/IR-01-051.pdf (Accessed 14 November 2022).

Oberthür, S. (2001) 'Linkages between the Montreal and Kyoto Protocols – Enhancing Synergies between Protecting the Ozone Layer and the Global Climate', *International Environmental Agreements*, 1(3), pp. 357–77. https://doi.org/10.1023/A:1011535823228.

OceanNETs (2022) *Ocean-based Negative Emissions Technologies.* www.oceannets.eu/ (Accessed 3 August 2022).

Oldham, P. et al. (2014) 'Mapping the Landscape of Climate Engineering', *Philosophical Transactions of the Royal Society A: Mathematical, Physical and Engineering Sciences*, 372(20140065), pp. 1–20. https://doi.org/10.1098/rsta.2014.0065.

Oomen, J. (2021) *Imagining Climate Engineering: Dreaming of the Designer Climate.* London: Routledge.

Oreskes, N. (2015) 'How Earth Science Has Become a Social Science', *Historical Social Research*, 40(2), pp. 246–70. https://doi.org/10.12759/hsr.40.2015.2.246-270.

Parker, C. F., Karlsson, C. and Hjerpe, M. (2017) 'Assessing the European Union's global climate change leadership: from Copenhagen to the Paris Agreement', *Journal of European Integration*, 39(2), pp. 239–52. https://doi.org/10.1080/07036337.2016.1275608.

Parson, E. A. (2014) 'Climate Engineering in Global Climate Governance: Implications for Participation and Linkage', *Transnational Environmental Law*, 3(01), pp. 89–110. https://doi.org/10.1017/S2047102513000496.

Petersen, A. (2014) 'The Emergence of the Geoengineering Debate Within the IPCC', *Geoengineeering our Climate Working Paper and Opinion Article Series*. http://wp.me/p2zsRk-bp.

Pielke, R. J. et al. (2007) 'Lifting the Taboo on Adaptation', *Nature*, 445 (February 2007), pp. 597–98.

Porter, K. E. and Hulme, M. (2013) 'The Emergence of the Geoengineering Debate in the UK Print Media: A Frame Analysis', *The Geographical Journal*, 179(4), pp. 342–55. https://doi.org/10.1111/geoj.12003.

President's Science Advisory Committee (1965) *Restoring the Quality of Our Environment*. Washington, DC: U.S. Government Printing Office.

Price, D. J. de S. (1983) *Little Science, Big Science ... and Beyond*. New York: Columbia University Press.

Rayner, S. et al. (2013) 'The Oxford Principles', *Climatic Change*, 121(3), pp. 499–512. https://doi.org/10.1007/s10584-012-0675-2.

Rogelj, J. et al. (2015) 'Zero Emission Targets as Long-Term Global Goals for Climate Protection', *Environmental Research Letters*, 10(105007), pp. 1–11. https://doi.org/10.1088/1748-9326/10/10/105007.

Saami Council (2021) *Regarding SCoPEx Plans for Test Flights at the Swedish Space Corporation in Kiruna, Open Letter*. https://static1.squarespace.com/static/5dfb35a66f00d54ab0729b75/t/603e2167a9c0b96ffb027c8d/1614684519754/Letter+to+Scopex+Advisory+Committee+24+February.pdf (Accessed 10 June 2021).

Sand, P. H. (2010) 'The Precautionary Principle: A European Perspective', *Human and Ecological Risk Assessment*, 6(3), pp. 445–58. https://doi.org/10.1080/10807030091124563.

Schelling, T. C. (1996) 'The Economic Diplomacy of Geoengineering', *Climatic Change*, 33, pp. 303–7. https://doi.org/10.1007/BF00142578.

Schneider, S. H. (1996) 'Geoengineering: Could – or Should –We do It?', *Climatic Change*, 33, pp. 291–302. https://doi.org/10.1007/BF00142577.

Schubert, J. (2021) *Engineering the Climate: Science, Politics, and Visions of Control*. Manchester, UK: Mattering Press.

Schubert, J. (2022) 'Science-State Alliances and Climate Engineering: A "Longue Durée" Picture', *Wiley Interdisciplinary Reviews: Climate Change*, 13(6), p. e801. https://doi.org/10.1002/WCC.801.

Seifert, E. K. and Bräker, S. (2020) 'Klimaschutz – im Fokus der internationalen Normung', *DIN Mitteilungen*, (April), pp. 105–14.

Shepherd, J. et al. (2009) *Geoengineering the Climate: Science, Governance and Uncertainty.* London: The Royal Society.

Stephens, J. C. and Surprise, K. (2020) 'The Hidden Injustices of Advancing Solar Geoengineering Research', *Global Sustainability*, 3(e2), pp. 1–6. https://doi.org/10.1017/sus.2019.28.

Stone, D. (2002) 'Introduction: Global Knowledge and Advocacy Networks', *Global Networks*, 2(1), pp. 1–11. https://doi.org/10.1111/1471-0374.00023.

Sugiyama, M., Asayama, S. and Kosugi, T. (2020) 'The North–South Divide on Public Perceptions of Stratospheric Aerosol Geoengineering?: A Survey in Six Asia-Pacific Countries', https://doi.org/10.1080/17524032.2019.1699137.

Sun, W. et al. (2020) 'Global Monsoon Response to Tropical and Arctic Stratospheric Aerosol Injection', *Climate Dynamics*, 55(7–8), pp. 2107–21. https://doi.org/10.1007/s00382-020-05371-7.

UNFCCC (1992) *United Nations Framework Convention on Climate Change.* https://unfccc.int/resource/docs/convkp/conveng.pdf (Accessed 9 March 2021).

U.S. House of Representatives (2010) *Engineering the Climate: Research Needs and Strategies for International Coordination Report.* Committee on Science and Technology, 111th Congress, 2nd Session, October. https://www.washingtonpost.com/wp-srv/nation/pdfs/Geongineeringreport.pdf (Accessed 14 November 2022)

van Beek, L. et al. (2020) 'Anticipating Futures through Models: The Rise of Integrated Assessment Modelling in the Climate Science-Policy Interface since 1970', *Global Environmental Change*, 65(102191), pp. 1–14. https://doi.org/10.1016/J.GLOENVCHA.2020.102191.

Van Den Belt, H. and Gremmen, B. (2002) 'Between Precautionary Principle and "Sound Science": Distributing the Burdens of Proof', *Journal of Agricultural and Environmental Ethics*, 15(1), pp. 103–22. https://doi.org/10.1023/A:1013862024432.

Van Vuuren, D. P. et al. (2018) 'Alternative Pathways to the 1.5 °C Target Reduce the Need for Negative Emission Technologies', *Nature Climate Change*, 8(5), pp. 391–7. https://doi.org/10.1038/s41558-018-0119-8.

Victor, D. G. et al. (2009) 'The Geoengineering Option – A Last Resort against Global Warming?' *Foreign Affairs*, 88(2), pp. 64–76. www.jstor.org/stable/20699494.

Whyte, K. P. (2019) 'Indigeneity in Geoengineering Discourses: Some Considerations', *Ethics, Policy & Environment*, 21(3), pp. 289–307. https://doi.org/10.1080/21550085.2018.1562529.

Witte, J. M., Reineke, W. H. and Benner, T. (2000) 'Beyond Multilateralism: Global Public Policy Networks', *Internationale Politik und Gesellschaft*, 2, pp. 176–88.

Workman, M. et al. (2020) 'Decision Making in Contexts of Deep Uncertainty – An Alternative Approach for Long-Term Climate Policy', *Environmental Science & Policy*, 103, pp. 77–84. https://doi.org/10.1016/J.ENVSCI.2019 .10.002.

Zalasiewicz, J. et al. (eds) (2019) *The Anthropocene as a Geological Time Unit: A Guide to the Scientific Evidence and Current Debate*. Cambridge: Cambridge University Press.

Zuccala, A. (2006) 'Modeling the Invisible College', *Journal of the American Society for Information Science and Technology*, 57(2), pp. 152–68. https:// doi.org/10.1002/asi.

About the Author

Ina Möller is an assistant professor at the Environmental Policy Group of Wageningen University in the Netherlands. She holds a PhD in political science and has a background in environmental and sustainability studies. Her research focuses on social dynamics at the climate science and policy interface, their effect on anticipatory climate governance, and how actors navigate, use, and shape environmental regimes.

Acknowledgements

The writing of this Element would not have been possible without the support of some important people. I want to thank Ruben Zondervan for introducing me to the world of geoengineering, Fariborz Zelli for giving me the opportunity to study it in depth, and Johannes Lindvall for teaching me to keep an eye on the bigger picture. I want to thank Frank Biermann for seeing the potential of my findings for questions of justice and Aarti Gupta for encouraging me to continue studying the politics of geoengineering. In this context, I also want to thank my colleagues and friends in the Earth System Governance Project who made the experience of becoming a researcher so special. A sincere thank you also goes to Michael Mason as series editor and two anonymous reviewers for helping me improve the manuscript for this Element. Finally, I want to express my gratitude to all those who shared their thoughts, opinions, and experiences with me during the course of my research.

Cambridge Elements ☰

Earth System Governance

Frank Biermann
Utrecht University

Frank Biermann is Research Professor of Global Sustainability Governance with the Copernicus Institute of Sustainable Development, Utrecht University, the Netherlands. He is the founding Chair of the Earth System Governance Project, a global transdisciplinary research network launched in 2009; and Editor-in-Chief of the new peer-reviewed journal *Earth System Governance* (Elsevier). In April 2018, he won a European Research Council Advanced Grant for a research program on the steering effects of the Sustainable Development Goals.

Aarti Gupta
Wageningen University

Aarti Gupta is Professor of Global Environmental Governance at Wageningen University, The Netherlands. She is Lead Faculty and a member of the Scientific Steering Committee of the Earth System Governance (ESG) Project and a Coordinating Lead Author of its 2018 Science and Implementation Plan. She is also principal investigator of the Dutch Research Council-funded TRANSGOV project on the Transformative Potential of Transparency in Climate Governance. She holds a PhD from Yale University in environmental studies.

Michael Mason
London School of Economics and Political Science (LSE)

Michael Mason is Associate Professor in the Department of Geography and Environment at the London School of Economics and Political Science (LSE). At LSE he also Director of the Middle East Centre and an Associate of the Grantham Institute on Climate Change and the Environment. Alongside his academic research on environmental politics and governance, he has advised various governments and international organisations on environmental policy issues, including the European Commission, ICRC, NATO, the UK Government (FCDO) and UNDP.

About the Series

Linked with the Earth System Governance Project, this exciting new series will provide concise but authoritative studies of the governance of complex socio-ecological systems, written by world-leading scholars. Highly interdisciplinary in scope, the series will address governance processes and institutions at all levels of decision-making, from local to global, within a planetary perspective that seeks to align current institutions and governance systems with the fundamental 21st Century challenges of global environmental change and earth system transformations.

Elements in this series will present cutting edge scientific research, while also seeking to contribute innovative transformative ideas towards better governance. A key aim of the series is to present policy-relevant research that is of interest to both academics and policy-makers working on earth system governance.

More information about the Earth System Governance project can be found at: www.earthsystemgovernance.org

Cambridge Elements ≡

Earth System Governance

Lightning Source UK Ltd.
Milton Keynes UK
UKHW021939090223
416794UK00011B/117